1000 THINGS
YOU SHOULD KNOW ABOUT

BUILDINGS & TRANSPORTATION

1000 THINGS YOU SHOULD KNOW ABOUT

BUILDINGS & TRANSPORTATION

John Farndon

Mason Crest
Publishers

Mason Crest Publishers Inc.
370 Reed Road, Broomall, PA 19008
(866) MCP-BOOK (toll free)
www.masoncrest.com
This edition first published in 2003

Miles Kelly Publishing,
Bardfield Centre, Great Bardfield, Essex, CM7 4SL, U.K.
Copyright © Miles Kelly Publishing 2000, 2003

2 4 6 8 10 9 7 5 3 1

Library of Congress Cataloging-in-Publication Data on file
at the Library of Congress

ISBN 1-59084-463-7

Editorial Director: Anne Marshall
Editors: Amanda Learmonth, Jenni Rainford
Assistant: Liberty Newton
Americanization: Cindy Leaney
Written and designed by: John Farndon and Angela Koo

Printed in China

CONTENTS

KEY

 Cars

 Trains

 Planes

 Buildings

 Great monuments

 Boats

Cathedrals

- **Cathedrals** are the churches of Christian bishops.

- **The word cathedral** comes from the Greek word for "seat" *kathedra*.

- **Cathedrals** are typically built in the shape of a cross. The entrance of the cathedral is at the west end.

- **The long end** of the cross is the nave.

▲ Paris's famous Notre Dame dates from 1163, but was remodeled in the 1840s by Viollet-le-Duc.

- The short end, containing the altar and choir stalls, is called the apse. The arms of the cross are called transepts.

- **Canterbury and a few other cathedrals** were built as early as the 6th century AD. Most European cathedrals were built between 1000 and 1500.

- **Medieval cathedrals** were often built in the "gothic" style with soaring, pointed arches, tall spires, and huge pointed arch windows.

- **Many gothic cathedrals** have beautiful stained-glass windows. Chartres Cathedral in France has 176.

- **The modern Crystal Cathedral** in California is star-shaped and made of glass for TV broadcasts.

- **The world's tallest** cathedral spire is in Ulm, Germany, which is 528ft (160.9m) tall.

- **The world's smallest** cathedral is Christ Church in Highlandville, Missouri, which is just 13.7ft (4.2m) by 17ft (5.2m) and holds only 18 people.

The first railroads

- **Railroads** were invented long before steam power.

- **The Diolkos** was a 4mi (6km) long railroad that transported boats across the Corinthisthmus in Greece in the 6th century BC. Trucks pushed by slaves ran in grooves in a limestone track.

- **The Diolkos** ran for over 1,300 years until AD900.

- **Railroads** in Europe were revived in the 14th century with wooden trackrails to guide horse and handcarts taking ore out of mines.

- **In the 1700s,** English ironmakers began to make rails of iron. First the rail was wood covered in iron. Then the whole rail was made of iron. Iron wheels with "flanges" (lips) ran inside the track.

▶ The Stephensons' Rocket was the most famous early locomotive, winning the first locomotive speed trials at Rainhill in England in 1829.

- **In 1804** English engineer Richard Trevithick built the first successful steam railroad locomotive.

- **Trevithick's** engine pulled a train of five wagons with 9 tons of iron and 70 men along 9mi (15km) of track at the Pendarren ironworks in Wales.

- **On September 27, 1825** George and Robert Stephenson opened the world's first steam passenger railroad, the Stockton and Darlington in England.

- **The gauge (trackwidth)** used for the Stockton and Darlington was 4.72ft (1.44m), the same length as axles on horsewagons. This became the standard gauge in the U.S. and much of Europe.

- **The English-built Stourbridge Lion** was the first full-size steam locomotive to run in the U.S. It ran on wooden track in Pennsylvania in 1829.

Controlling a plane

- **A plane** is controlled in the air by moving hinged flaps on its wings and tail.
- **Changing pitch** is when the plane goes nose-up or nose-down to dive or climb.
- **Rolling** is when the plane rolls to one side, dipping one wing or the other.
- **Yawing** is when the plane steers to the left or right like a car.
- **Pitch** is controlled by raising or lowering hinged flaps on the rear wings called elevators.
- **To pitch up** in a small or simple plane, the pilot pulls back on the control column to raise the elevators.
- **Rolling** is controlled by large hinged flaps on the wings called ailerons.

◄ In old-fashioned planes, the pilot controlled the flaps manually by moving a control stick linked to the flaps by cables. In modern planes, the flaps are controlled automatically via electric wires (fly-by-wire) or laser beams (fly-by-light). The flight deck of this plane from 30 years ago has lots of dials to help the pilot. Modern planes have "glass cockpits," which means they have computer screens.

- **To roll left,** the pilot pushes the control column to the left, which raises the aileron on the left wing and lowers it on the right.
- **Yawing** is controlled by the vertical hinged flap on the tail called the rudder.
- **To yaw left,** the pilot pushes the foot-operated rudder bar forward with his left foot, to swing the rudder left.

Trucks

- **Trucks** can weigh 40 tons or more—maybe as much as 50 automobiles.
- **Cars** are powered by gasoline engines; trucks are typically powered by diesel engines.
- **Cars** typically have five forward gears; trucks often have as many as 16.
- **Cars** typically have four wheels. Trucks often have 12 or 16 to help spread the load.
- **Many trucks** have the same basic cab and chassis (the framework supporting the body). Different bodies are fitted on to the chassis to suit the load.
- **Some trucks** are in two parts, hinged at the join. These are called trailer trucks.
- **The cab and engine** of a trailer truck is called the tractor unit. The load is carried in the trailer.
- **In Australia** one tractor may pull several trailers in a "road-train" along the long, straight desert roads.

▲ This 14-wheel tanker is a trailer truck—the tank and tractor unit can be separated.

- **The longest truck** is the Arctic Snow Train, first made for the U.S. army—570ft (174m) long with 54 wheels.
- **Large trucks** are sometimes called "juggernauts." Juggernaut was a form of the Hindu god Vishnu who rode a huge chariot, supposed by Europeans to crush people beneath its wheels.

Mosques

- **The word "mosque"** comes from the Arabic *masjid*, which means a place of kneeling.

- **Mosques** are places where Muslims worship. Muslims can worship anywhere clean. So a mosque can be just a stick in the sand to mark out a space for praying or even just a mat. But many mosques are beautiful buildings.

- **Cathedral or Friday** mosques are large

▲ *Typically minarets on mosques have onion-shaped roofs.*

mosques big enough to hold all the adult Muslims in the area.

- **Typically** mosques have a courtyard surrounded by four walls called iwans. There is often a fountain or fuawara at the center for ceremonial washing.

- **The mihrab** is a decorative niche on the inner wall closest to the city of Mecca that Muslims face when praying.

- **The mimbar** is the stone or wooden pulpit where the Imam, chief officer, leads the people in prayer.

- **Most mosques** have two to six tall pointed towers which are called minarets.

- **On each minaret** is a balcony from which muezzin (criers) call the faithful to prayer five times a day.

- **Minarets** may have been inspired by the Pharos, the famous lighthouse at Alexandria in Egypt.

- **There are** no paintings or statues in mosques, only abstract patterns, often made of tiles.

Motorcycles

▲ *Many enthusiasts still ride motorcycles like this from the 1930s when motorcycling was in its heyday.*

- **The first gasoline engine** motorcycle was built by Gottlieb Daimler in Germany in 1885.

- **Most small motorcycles** have a two-stroke gasoline engine, typically air-cooled and quite noisy.

- **Most larger motorcycles** have four-stroke gasoline engines, typically watercooled.

- **On most bikes** the engine drives the rear wheel through a chain; on some the drive is through a shaft.

- **A trail bike** is a bike with a high mounted frame and chunky tires, designed to be ridden over rough tracks.

- **In Britain,** motorcycles with engines smaller than 50cc may be called mopeds, because in the past they had pedals as well as an engine.

- **The biggest motorcycles** have engines of about 1200cc.

- **The most famous** motorcycle race in the world is the Isle of Man TT, or Tourist Trophy.

- **In Speedway,** bikes with no brakes or gears are raced round dirt tracks.

> ★ STAR FACT ★
> The first motorcycle was steam-powered, and built by the Michaux brothers in 1868.

Building the railroads

- **On September 15, 1830** the world's first real passenger railroad opened between Liverpool and Manchester.

- **At the opening** of the Liverpool and Manchester railroad, government minister William Huskisson was the first casualty, killed by the locomotive.

- **In 1831** the *Best Friend* started a regular train service between Charleston and Hamburg, South Carolina.

- **By 1835** there were over 1000mi of railroad in the U.S.

- **In Britain,** railroad building became a mania in the 1840s.

- **Hundreds of Acts of Parliament** gave railroad companies the powers to carve their way through cities and the countryside.

◀ *The new railroads often meant demolishing huge strips through cities.*

- **By the late 1840s** Great Western Railway trains were able to average well over 60mph (100km/h) all the way from London to Exeter via Bristol, completing the 180mi (300km) journey in under four hours.

- **On May 10th, 1869** railroads from either side of the U.S. met at Promontory, Utah, giving North America the first transcontinental railroad.

- **The British** built 24,000mi (40,000km) of railroads in India in the 1880s.

- **Vast armies of men** helped build the railroads—45,000 on the London and Southampton railroad alone.

Early boats

- **The Aborigines** arrived by boat in Australia at least 50,000 years ago, as cave paintings show.

- **The oldest boat remains** are 8,000 or so years old, like the 13ft (4m) canoe found at Pesse in the Netherlands.

- **Many early canoes** were simply hollowed out logs, called dugouts.

- **The islands of the Pacific** were probably colonized by dugouts, stabilized by attaching an outrigger (an extra float on the side) or adding extra hulls.

- **Lighter canoes** could be made by stretching animal skins over a light frame of bent wood.

- **4,000 years ago,** ancient Egyptians were constructing ships over 100ft (30m) long by interlocking planks of wood and lashing them together with tough grass rope.

- **By 1000BC,** Phoenician traders were sailing into the Atlantic in ships made of Cedar of Lebanon trees.

▲◀ *Outriggers (above) were used to colonize the Pacific tens of thousands of years ago. But many early boats like the Welsh coracle (left) were made by stretching animal skins over a wooden frame.*

- **All early boats** were driven by hand, using either a pole pushed along the bottom, or a paddle.

- **Sails** were used for the first time 7,000 years ago in Mesopotamia on reed trading boats.

- **The first known picture** of a sail is 5,500 years old and comes from Egypt.

Castles

- **Castles** were the fortress homes of powerful men, such as kings and dukes, in the Middle Ages. The castle acted as a stronghold for commanding the country around it. They were also barracks for troops, prisons, armories, and centers of local government.

- **The first castles,** in the 11th century, had a high earth mound called a motte, topped by a wooden tower. Around this was an enclosure called a bailey, protected by a fence of wooden stakes and a ditch.

- **From the 12th century** the tower was built of stone and called a keep or donjon. This was the last refuge in an attack. Soon the wooden fences were replaced by thick stone walls and strong towers.

- **Walls and towers** were topped by battlements—low walls with gaps for defenders to fire weapons from.

- **Castles evolved** from a simple square tower to elaborate rings of fortifications. The entrance or gatehouse was equipped with booby traps.

- **From the 13th century** the ditch around the castle was often dug deep, filled with water, and called a moat. This stopped enemies from sapping (digging under the walls).

- **Many castles** in England and Wales were first built by the Norman conquerors in the 11th century, including Windsor Castle which dates from 1070.

- **In early castles** there was just a single great hall. Later castles had extra small rooms for the lord and lady, such as the solar, which had windows.

- **The gong farmer** was the man who had to clean out the pit at the bottom of the garderobe (toilet shute).

- **An attack on a castle** was called a siege and could last many months, or even years.

▼ This shows some of the main features of a medieval castle. Very few castles had all of these features. Innovations were constantly being added over the centuries as attackers came up with better ways of breaching the defenses and defenders found ways to hold them at bay.

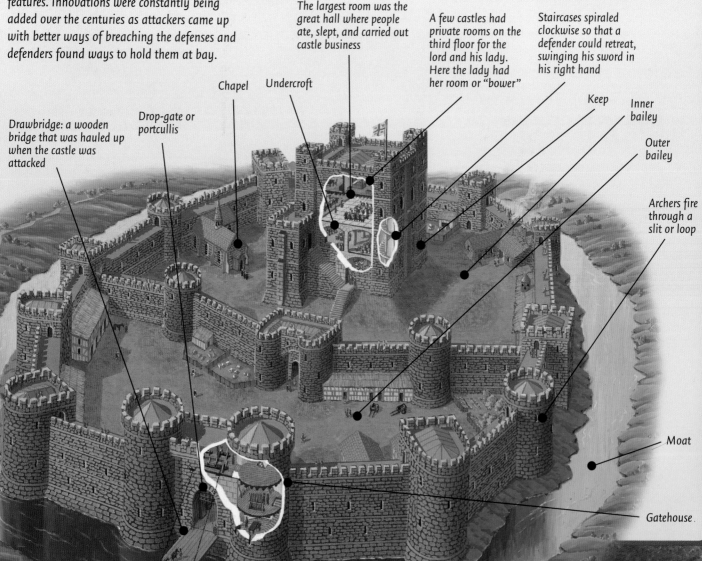

The largest room was the great hall where people ate, slept, and carried out castle business

A few castles had private rooms on the third floor for the lord and his lady. Here the lady had her room or "bower"

Staircases spiraled clockwise so that a defender could retreat, swinging his sword in his right hand

Chapel

Undercroft

Keep

Inner bailey

Drawbridge: a wooden bridge that was hauled up when the castle was attacked

Drop-gate or portcullis

Outer bailey

Archers fire through a slit or loop

Moat

Gatehouse

Galleons

◄ In this replica of a ship from around 1600, the tall stern castle where the captain lived is clearly visible.

- **Galleons** were huge sailing ships that were built from the mid-1500s onward.
- **Galleons** had tall structures called castles at either end.
- **The front castle** was called the forecastle or fo'c'sle (said folk-sel).
- **The rear castle** was called the stern castle and it housed elaborate living quarters for the officers.

The crew lived in crowded rows below deck.

- **The stern of the ship** was often ornately carved, decorated in gold, and painted bright colors.
- **A galleon** had three tall masts: the foremast, the mainmast, and the mizzenmast at the rear.
- **Galleons** were both warships and trading boats and carried large numbers of cannon and troops.
- **In the 1500s,** huge Spanish galleons crossed the Atlantic carrying gold from the Americas to Spain.
- **When the Spanish Armada** of galleons was sent to attack England in 1588, they were defeated by the smaller but faster and lighter English ships, despite their heavy armament.

> ★ STAR FACT ★
> The biggest Spanish galleons weighed well over 1,000 tons.

The Colosseum

- **The Colosseum** was a huge stone sports arena built in Ancient Rome.
- **It was 620ft (189m) long,** 510ft (156m) wide, and 170ft (52m) high.
- **It held** about 50,000 spectators who entered through 80 entrances.
- **The sports** included fights between gladiators with swords, nets, and other weapons who fought to the death. They also fought against wild beasts.
- **Counterweighted** doors allowed 64 wild beasts to be released from their cages simultaneously.
- **It took just eight years**—from around AD70–AD78—to build the entire structure of the Colosseum.
- **To build** it the Romans brought almost a quarter of a million tons of stone by barge from quarries 12mi (20km) outside Rome.
- **During construction**, a cart carrying a ton of stone would have left the riverside wharves every seven

▲ The Colosseum in Rome was one of the greatest buildings of the ancient world.

minutes on the 1mi (1.5km) journey to the site.

- **A huge awning** called a velarium, supported by 240 masts, protected the arena from bad weather.
- **Its opening was celebrated** by spectacular games lasting 100 days.

Tractors

- **Tractors** are motor vehicles used mostly on farms for pulling or pushing machines such as plows.

- **Tractors** are also used in factories, by the army, for logging and for clearing snow.

- **Steam-powered tractors** called "traction engines" were introduced in 1834 by Walter Hancock.

- **Traction-engines** could pull up to 40 plows at once via long chains, but they were too cumbersome to be practical in hilly country.

- **Gasoline-powered tractors** were introduced in the 1890s but they were not powerful enough for most farm work.

- **The first all-purpose** farm tractors appeared in the 1920s and soon began to replace horses and oxen.

> ★ STAR FACT ★
> There are now well over 16 million tractors around the world.

▲ *Modern tractors can be adapted to operate all kinds of devices, including this haybaler, via the power takeoff.*

- **Plows and other equipment** are drawn along via the towbar on the back of the tractor.

- **The power take-off** or PTO allows the tractor's engine to power equipment such as potato diggers.

- **25 percent of all tractors** are in the U.S.

The Age of sail

- **East Indiamen** were ships that carried ivory, silks, and spices to Europe from India, China, and the East Indies.

- **By 1800** Indiamen could carry 1,000 tons of cargo.

- **Packet ships** were ships that provided a regular service across the Atlantic between Europe and the U.S.—they sailed regardless of whether they had a full load or not.

- **The first packet service** began in 1818 with the Black Ball Line from Liverpool to New York. Red Star and Swallowtail followed.

◀ *The tea clippers of the mid-1800s were the pinnacle of sailing ship technology, able to carry thousands of tons of tea at speeds of 20 knots or more.*

- **Clippers** were the big, fast sailing ships that "clipped off" time as they raced to get cargoes of tea from China and India back first to markets in Europe and the U.S.

- **Clippers** had slender hulls, tall masts, and up to 35 sails.

- **Clippers could reach** speeds of 30 knots (35mph/ 55km/h). Many could sail from New York, around South America, to San Francisco in under 100 days.

- **In 1866** the clippers *Taeping*, *Serica*, and *Ariel* raced 15,970mi (25,700km) from Foochow in China to London in 99 days.

- **Canadian Donald Mckay** of Boston, Massachusetts, was the greatest clipper builder. His ship the *Great Republic* of 1853 was the biggest ship of its time, over 350ft (100m) long and able to carry 4,000 tons of cargo.

- **A famous clipper,** the *Cutty Sark*, built in 1869 is preserved at Greenwich, London. Its name is Scottish for "short shirt" and comes from the witch in Robert Burns's poem *Tam O'Shanter*.

Parachutes, hang gliders

- **Leonardo da Vinci** drew a design for a parachute around 1500.
- **The first human parachute drop** was made by Jacques Garnerin from a balloon over Paris in 1797.
- **Folding parachutes** were used first in the United States in 1880.
- **Early parachutes** were made of canvas, then silk. Modern parachutes are made of nylon, stitched in panels to limit tears to a small area.
- **Until recently** parachutes were shaped like umbrellas; now most are "parafoils"—wing-shaped.
- **Drogues** are parachutes thrown out by jet planes and high-speed cars to slow them down.
- **German Otto Lilienthal** flew his own canvas and wood hang-gliders in the 1890s.
- **Modern hang gliding** began with the fabric delta

◀ Parachutes are widely used in modern naval exersises as demonstrated by this U.S. Navy SEAL.

(triangular) wing design developed by the American Francis Rogallo in the 1940s.

- **Today's hang gliders** are made by stretching nylon over a very light and strong nylon and kevlar frame. They combine long airplane-like wings and a double skin of fabric to achieve very long flights.
- **The first hang gliders** achieved a glide ratio of 1:2.5, that is, they traveled only 8ft (2.5m) forward for every 3ft (1m) that they dropped. Today's hang-gliders give glide ratios of 1:14 or better.

Skyscrapers

- **The first skyscrapers** were built in Chicago and New York in the 1880s.
- **A crucial step** in the development of skyscrapers was the invention of the fast safety elevator in 1857.
- **The Home Insurance Building** in Chicago, built in 1885, was one of the first skyscrapers.
- **In buildings** over 40 stories high, the weight of the building is less important in terms of strength than the wind load (force of the wind against the building).
- **The Empire State Building,** built in New York in 1931, was for decades the world's tallest building at 1,250ft (381m).
- **In 2002, the tallest building** in the U.S. was the 1,450ft (442m) high Sears Tower in Chicago.

▶ New York's Manhattan has more skyscrapers than anywhere else in the world.

- **The world's tallest building** is the 1,450ft (442m) Petronas twin towers in Kuala Lumpur, Malaysia.
- **A tower** being built in Sao Paolo in Brazil may be the world's tallest at 1,625ft (495m).
- **If the Grollo Tower** is built in Melbourne, Australia, it will be 1,840ft (560m) tall.

> **! NEWS FLASH !**
> The Landmark Tower in Kowloon, Hong Kong, could be 1,880ft (574m) high.

St. Sophia

- **St. or Hagia Sophia** was built as a Christian cathedral in Istanbul in Turkey ("Roman Byzantium").

- **Hagia Sophia** is Greek for "holy wisdom."

- **St. Sophia** was built between AD532 and 537, when Istanbul was called Constantinople.

- **The great Byzantine** emperor Justinian I ordered the building of St. Sophia after a fire destroyed an earlier church on the site.

- **St. Sophia** was designed by the brilliant Byzantine architects Anthemius of Tralles and Isidorus of Miletus.

- **The main structure** is a framework of arches and vaults (high arched ceilings).

- **The dome** is 102ft (31m) across and 184ft (56m) high. It is supported by four triangular brick pillars called pendentives.

- **St. Sophia is decorated** with marble veneers and mosaics of Mary, Christ, angels, and bishops.

- **In 1453** the Ottoman Turks took the city and converted St. Sophia to a mosque. They plastered over the mosaics and added four minarets on the outside.

- **In 1935** St. Sophia was converted into a museum and the mosaics were uncovered.

▼ *Istanbul's St. Sophia is one of the world's oldest cathedrals.*

Viking longships

- **Viking longships** were the long narrow boats built by the Viking warriors of Scandinavia around AD1000.

- **A virtually** intact ship was found in 1880 at Gokstad near Oseberg in Norway. A king was buried inside it.

- **Longships** were very fast, light, and

▲ *The Gokstad ship dates from c.AD900.*

seaworthy. They carried the Viking explorer Leif Ericsson across the Atlantic to North America.

- **In 1893** a replica of the Gokstad ship sailed across the Atlantic in 28 days.

- **Some Viking longships** were up to 100ft (30m) long and 55ft (17m) across and could carry 200 warriors.

- **At sea** longships relied on a single, large square sail made up from strips of woolen cloth. On rivers they used oarpower, with 20 to 30 rowers on each side.

- **The special design of their ships** allowed the Vikings to make raids far up shallow rivers.

- **The prow curved** up to a carved dragon head.

- **Longships** were for carrying warriors on raids, but the Vikings also built wider, deeper "knarrs" for trade and small rowing boats called "faerings."

- **The Viking** ships were very stable because they had a keel, a wooden board about 55ft (17m) long and 18in (45cm) deep, along the bottom of the boat.

Diesel trains

> ★ STAR FACT ★
> In 1987, a British Rail diesel train set a world diesel speed record of 150mph (240 km/h).

- **The diesel engine** was invented by Rudolf Diesel in 1892 and experiments with diesel locomotives started soon after. The first great success was the *Flying Hamburger* which ran from Berlin to Hamburg in the 1930s at speeds of 78mph (125km/h). Diesel took over from steam in the 1950s and 1960s.

- **Diesel locomotives** are really electric locomotives that carry their own power plant. The wheels are driven by an electric motor which is supplied with electricity by the locomotive's diesel engine.

- **The power output of a diesel** engine is limited, so high-speed trains are electric. However, diesels can supply their own electricity so need no trackside cables.

- **There are two other kinds** of diesel apart from diesel-electrics: diesel-hydraulic and diesel-mechanical.

- **In diesel-hydraulics,** the power from the diesel engine is connected to the wheels via a torque converter, which is a turbine driven around by fluid.

- **In diesel-mechanicals,** the power is transmitted from the diesel engine to the wheels via gears and shafts. This only works for small locomotives.

- **Diesel locomotives** may be made up of one or more separate units. An A unit holds the driver's cab and leads the train. A B unit simply holds an engine.

- **A typical diesel locomotive** for fast, heavy trains, or for trains going over mountains may consist of one A unit and six B units.

- **The usual maximum** power output from a single diesel locomotive is about 3,500–4,000 horsepower.

▼ This is a typical British diesel-electric locomotive from the 1960s. It has a cab at both ends so that it can be operated in either direction. This is one of the older generation of diesel-electrics that use DC (Direct Current) generators. DC generators give a current that flows in only one direction. Most newer engines take advantage of electronic devices called rectifiers to use the current from an AC (Alternating Current) generator. An AC generator gives a current that swaps direction many times a second. The rectifiers convert this into a direct current. AC generators are far more powerful and efficient.

Diesel engine in which diesel fuel is squeezed inside cylinders until it bursts into flame. The expansion of the fuel as it burns provides the engine's power

Fuel tank carrying diesel fuel. Because a diesel train carries its fuel on board, it is entirely independent, unlike electric locomotives

Cooling fan

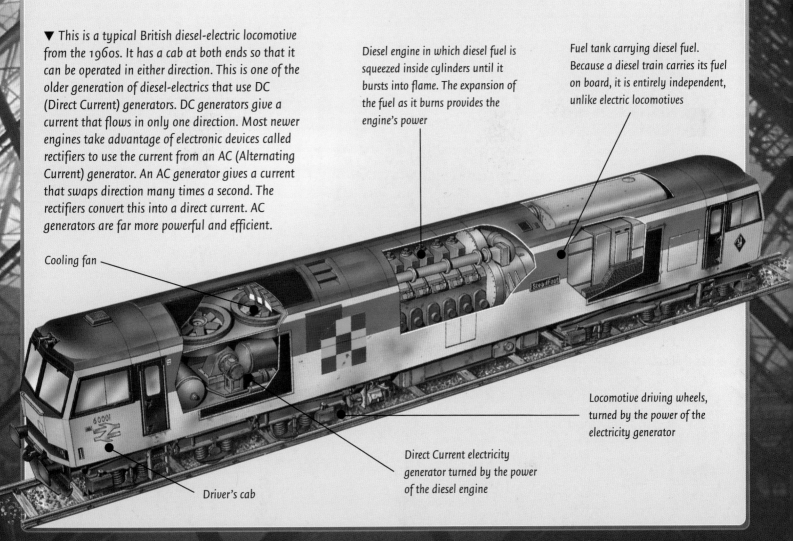

Locomotive driving wheels, turned by the power of the electricity generator

Direct Current electricity generator turned by the power of the diesel engine

Driver's cab

Supersonic planes

▶ In 1976 Concorde became the first supersonic aircraft to carry passengers on commercial flights. It is still in operation today.

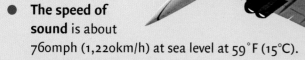

- **Supersonic planes** travel faster than the speed of sound.

- **The speed of sound** is about 760mph (1,220km/h) at sea level at 59°F (15°C).

- **Sound travels** slower high up, so the speed of sound is about 670mph (1,060km/h) at 40,000ft (12,000m).

- **Supersonic** plane speeds are given in Mach numbers. These are the speed of the plane divided by the speed of sound at the plane's altitude.

- **A plane flying** at 9,320mph (1,500km/h) at 40,000ft

! NEWS FLASH !
Spaceplanes of the near future may reach speeds of Mach 15.

(12,000m), where the speed of sound is 670mph (1,060km/h), is at Mach 1.46.

- **A plane flying** at supersonic speeds builds up shock waves in front and behind because it keeps catching up and compressing the soundwaves in front of it.

- **The double shock waves** create a sharp crack called a sonic boom that is heard on the ground.

- **In 1947** Chuck Yeager of the USAF made the first supersonic flight in the Bell X-1 rocket plane. The X-15 rocket plane later reached speeds faster than Mach 6. Speeds faster than Mach 5 are called hypersonic.

- **The first jet plane** to fly supersonic was the F-100 Super Saber fighter of 1953. The first supersonic bomber was the USAF's Convair B-58 Hustler of 1956.

Famous castles

▲ Eilean Donan in Scotland was used in the film Braveheart.

- **The Arab Gormaz Castle** in the Castile region of Spain is Western Europe's biggest and oldest castle. It was started in AD956 by Caliph Al-Hakam II. It is 0.6mi (1km) round and over 1,300ft (400m) across.

- **Bran Castle** in Romania was built in 1212 by Teutonic (German) knights. In the 1450s, it was one of the castles of Vlad the Impaler, the original Count Dracula.

- **Windsor Castle** in England has been one of the main homes of English kings and queens since the 1100s.

- **Malbork Castle** near Gdansk in Poland is the biggest medieval castle, built by the Teutonic knights in 1309.

- **Germany's Neuschwanstein** castle was started in 1869 by "Mad" King Ludwig II. Its name means "new swan castle" after the Swan Knight in Wagner's opera Lohengrin.

- **Neuschwanstein** is the model for the castle in Walt Disney's cartoon film Sleeping Beauty.

- **15th century Blarney Castle** in Ireland is home to the famous "Blarney stone." Kissing the stone is said to give people the "gift of the gab" (fast and fluent talk).

- **Tintagel Castle** in Cornwall, England, is where legend says the mythical King Arthur was conceived.

- **Colditz Castle** in Germany was a notorious prison camp in World War II.

- **Carcassone** in southern France is a town fortified by Catholics in 1220 against those of the Cathar religion.

Golden Gate Bridge

- **The Golden Gate Bridge** spans the entrance to San Francisco Bay in California.

- **The Golden Gate Bridge** is one of the world's largest suspension bridges.

- **The total length** of the bridge is 8,980ft (2,737m).

◀ San Francisco's Golden Gate Bridge is one of the busiest bridges in the world.

! NEWS FLASH !
The tower's foundations are being reinforced to withstand earthquakes.

- **The towers** at either end are 1,115ft (340m) high. The suspended span between the towers is 4,200ft (1,280m), one of the longest in the world.

- **The roadway is** 220ft (67m) above the water, although this varies according to the tide

- **The Golden Gate Bridge** was designed by Joseph Baerman Strauss and built for $35 million, a third of the original cost estimate.

- **The bridge** was opened to traffic on May 27, 1937.

- **The bridge** carries two six-lane highways and pedestrian paths.

- **Unusually,** the bridge is double deck, carrying traffic one way on the upper deck and the other way on the lower deck.

Junks

- **Junks** are wooden sailing boats that have been used in China and the Far East for thousands of years.

- **Typical junks** have a broad flat bow (front).

- **Typical junks** have a broad, high stern castle (rear).

- **Junks have lugsails**. These are triangular sails arranged almost in line with the boat, allowing the boat to sail almost into the wind—unlike the square sails of early European boats which only worked with the wind behind.

- **The Chinese** are believed to have invented lugsails.

- **By the 1400s,** the Chinese were building junks 490ft (150m) long and almost 330ft (100m) wide—much bigger than any sailing ship yet built in Europe.

- **In 1405** the Chinese admiral Cheng Ho led a fleet of exploration through the Indian Ocean. His fleet consisted of 62 large junks and 255 small junks. Each of the large junks was gigantic compared with Columbus's *Santa Maria*. The biggest junk was over 1,500 tons—the *Santa Maria* was only 98 tons.

- **Between 1790 and 1810,** traders in the South Seas were terrorized by vast fleets of pirate junks, led by the female pirate Cheng I Sao.

- **Nowadays** most junks are motorized.

- **Junks** are often moored permanently as homes.

▶ Most sailing junks have two or three masts. Some have more. The sails are made from cotton and supported by bamboo struts.

Fighters of World War II

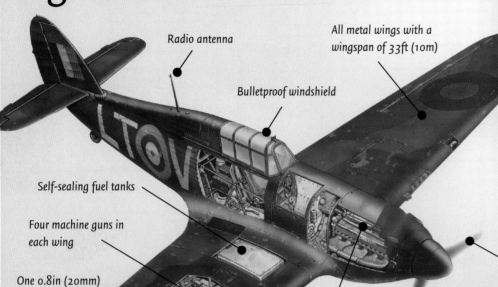

Radio antenna

All metal wings with a wingspan of 33ft (10m)

Bulletproof windshield

Self-sealing fuel tanks

Four machine guns in each wing

One 0.8in (20mm) cannon in each wing

1030 hp Rolls-Royce Merlin engine capable of powering the plane to over 325mph (520km/h)

Three-blade propeller

◀ Along with the Spitfire, the Hurricane was the mainstay of the British defense against the German air invasion in the Battle of Britain in 1940. Hurricanes and Spitfires would have spectacular aerial "dogfights" with the Me 109s escorting the German bombers. The sturdy Hurricane proved a highly effective fighter plane.

> ★ **STAR FACT** ★
> The "Night Witches" were a crack Soviet squadron of female fighter pilots who flew night raids on the Germans in the Caucasus Mountains.

▲ In the dogfights of the Battle of Britain, the Spitfire's 400mph (650km/h) top speed and amazing agility proved decisive.

- **World War II** fighter planes were sleek monoplanes (single-winged aircraft) very different from the biplanes of World War I. Many were developed from racing machines of the 1920s and 1930s.

- **The most famous** British plane was the Supermarine Spitfire. This was developed from the S.6B seaplane which won the coveted Schneider trophy in the late 1920s.

- **The most famous American** fighter was the North American P-51 Mustang, which could reach speeds of over 435mph (700km/h) and had a range of 1,000mi (1,700km). It was widely used as an escort for bombers.

- **In the Pacific** U.S. planes like the Grumman Wildcat and Hellcat fought against the fast and highly maneuverable Japanese Mitsubishi A6M "Zero."

- **The most famous German** fighter was the fast, agile Messerschmidt Bf 109. This was the plane flown by German air ace Erich Hartmann, who shot down 352 enemy planes. Over 33,000 were made during the war.

- **Me 109s** were nicknamed by model. The Bf109E was the Emil. The Bf109G was the Gustav.

- **The German Focke-Wulf 190** had a big BMW radial engine that let it climb over 685mi (1,100m) a minute.

- **The most famous Soviet** fighter was the MiG LaGG-3 Interceptor, flown by Soviet air ace Ivan Kozhedub who shot down 62 German planes.

- **The British Hawker Hurricane** was more old-fashioned, slower, and less famous than the Spitfire, but its reliability made it highly effective. Hurricanes actually destroyed more enemy aircraft than Spitfires.

The Benz

- **Karl Benz (1844–1929)** and his wife Berta were the German creators of the first successful gasoline-powered car in 1885.

- **At the age of 16,** before Lenoir built his gasoline-powered cart, Karl Benz dreamed of "a unit that could supplant the steam engine."

- **Karl and Berta Benz** began developing their car in the 1870s, while trying to earn money from a tin-making business. By 1880, they were so penniless they could barely afford to eat everyday.

- **Their first car** was a small tricycle, but had a water-cooled four-stroke engine with electric ignition.

▶ *The Benz tricycle was the world's first successful gasoline-powered car.*

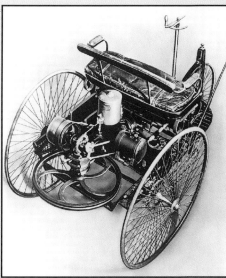

- **Karl Benz** tested the car around the streets of their home town of Mannheim after dark to avoid scaring people.

- **Berta Benz** recharged the car's battery after each trip by pedaling a dynamo attached to her sewing machine.

- **Berta Benz** secretly made the first long, 60mi (100km) journey in the car, without Karl knowing. On the journey to her home in Pforzheim, she had to clear the fuel line with a hairpin and use her garters to cure an electrical short.

- **The Benz** caused a stir when shown at the Paris World Fair in 1889.

- **Backed by F. von Fischer** and Julian Ganss, Benz began making his cars for sale in 1889—the first cars ever made for sale.

- **By 1900** Benz was making over 600 cars a year.

Stonehenge

- **Stonehenge** is an ancient stone monument in southern England made from circles of huge rough-cut stones.

- **The main circle of stones** or "sarsens" is a ring of 30 huge upright stones, joined at the top by 30 lintels. Many of these sarsens have now fallen or been looted.

- **Inside the sarsen ring** are five "doorways" called trilithons, each made with three gigantic stones, weighing up to 40 tons each.

- **In between** are rings of smaller bluestones.

- **The bluestones** come from the Preseli Hills in Wales, 150mi (240km) away. Archeologists puzzle over how they were carried here.

▶ *Experiments have shown a team of 150 people could haul the stones upright, but dragging them to the site on greased wooden sleds must have been a huge undertaking.*

- **At the center** is a single tall stone, called the Heel Stone.

- **Stonehenge was built** in three phases between 2950BC and 1600BC, starting with just a huge earth ring.

- **Archeologists** believe it was a gathering place and a site for religious ceremonies for Bronze Age people.

- **Newman, Thom, and Hawkins** have shown the layout of the stones ties in with astronomical events.

- **At sunrise on midsummer's day** (the solstice), the sun shines directly along the avenue to the Heel Stone.

Warplanes

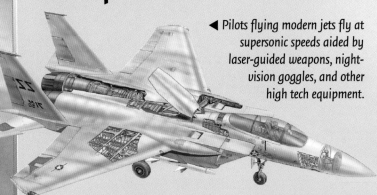

◀ Pilots flying modern jets fly at supersonic speeds aided by laser-guided weapons, night-vision goggles, and other high tech equipment.

- **The 540mph (870km/h)** German Messerschmidt Me 262 was the first jet fighter. It had straight wings.

- **The Lockheed Shooting Star** was the first successful U.S. jet fighter.

- **The Korean War** of the 1950s saw the first major combat between jet fighters. Most now had swept-back wings, like the Russian MiG-15 and the U.S. F-86 Saber.

- **In 1954** Boeing introduced the B-52 Superfortress, still the USAF's main bomber due to its huge capacity.

- **In the 1950s** aircraft began flying close to the ground to avoid detection by radar. On modern planes like the Lockheed F-111 a computer radar system flies the plane automatically at a steady height over hills and valleys. If the system fails, the plane climbs automatically.

- **The Hawker Harrier** of 1968 was the only successful "jump jet" with swiveling jets for vertical takeoff (VTOL).

- **Airborne Early Warning** systems (AEWs) look down from above and detect low-flying aircraft. To evade them, the U.S. began developing "stealth" systems like RCS.

- **RCS** (Radar Cross Section) means altering the plane's shape so it is less obvious to radar. RAM (Radar Absorbent Material) is a coating that won't reflect radar.

- **In 1988** the U.S. unveiled its first "stealth" bomber, the B-2, codenamed Have Blue. The F117 stea!th fighter followed.

- **The 1,550mph (2,500km/h)** Russian Sukhoi S-37 Berkut ("golden eagle") of 1997 uses Forward Swept Wings (FSW) for agility, rather than stealth technology.

Gears

▲ Gears are used in a huge range of machines, from watches to motorcycles, for transmitting movement from one shaft to another.

- **Gears** are pairs of toothed wheels that interlock and so transmit power from one shaft to another.

- **The first gears** were wooden, with wooden teeth. By the 6th century AD, wooden gears of all kinds were used in windmills, watermills, and winches.

- **Metal gears** appeared in 87BC and were later used for clocks. Today, all gears are metal and made on a "gear-hobbing" machine.

- **Simple gears** are wheels with straight cut teeth.

- **Helical gears** have slanting rather than straight teeth, and run smoother. The gears in cars are helical.

- **Bevel or miter gears** are cone-shaped, allowing shafts to interlock at right angles.

- **In worm gears** one big helical gear interlocks with a long spiral gear on a shaft at right angles.

- **Planetary gears** have gear wheels called spurs or planets that rotate around a central "sun" gear.

- **In a planetary gear** the planet and sun gear all rotate within a ring called an annulus.

> ★ STAR FACT ★
> Automatic gearboxes in cars use planetary or epicyclic gears.

Arches

- **Before arches,** door openings were just two uprights spanned by a straight piece of wood or stone called a lintel.

- **Arches** replace a straight lintel with a curve. Curved arches can take more weight than a lintel, as downward weight makes a lintel snap.

- **The Romans** were the first to use round arches, so round arches are called Roman or Romanesque arches.

- **Roman arches** were built from wedge-shaped blocks of stone called voussoirs. They were built up from each side on a semicircular wooden frame (later removed). A central wedge or keystone is slotted in at the top to hold them together.

- **The posts** supporting arches are called piers. The top of each post is called a springer.

◄ The famous Arc de Triomphe in Paris was commissioned by Napoleon in 1806 in the style of the triumphal arches built in Ancient Rome to celebrate great victories.

- **Pointed arches** were first used in Arab mosques like the Dome of the Rock in the 7th century.

- **Pointed arches** were brought to Europe from the Middle East by Crusader knights in the 1100s and put in churches to become part of the gothic style.

- **Horseshoe arches** are used in Islamic buildings all around the world.

- **The sides** of an ogee arch are S-shaped. Tudor arches are flattened ogee arches.

- **The world's biggest free-standing arch** is the Gateway to the West in St. Louis, Missouri. Completed in 1965, this arch is 630ft (192m) high and 630ft (192m) across.

Record-breaking trains

- **The fastest steam train** ever was the *Mallard*, at a speed of 125mph (201km/h) in 1938.

- **The most powerful** steam locomotive was the U.S. Virginian Railway No.700. It pulled with a force of over 198,416lb (90,000kg).

- **The heaviest trains** ever pulled by a single locomotive were 250-truck trains that ran on the Erie Railroad from 1914 to 1929. They weighed over 15,000 tons.

- **The longest train** was a 4.5mi (7.3km) 660-truck train that ran from Saldanha to Sishen in South Africa in 1989.

- **The longest passenger train** was a 5,682ft (1,732m) 70-car train from Ghent to Ostend, Belgium, in 1991.

- **The fastest diesel train** was 454mph (248km/h) by a British Rail Intercity from Darlington to York in 1987.

- **The fastest scheduled service** is the Hiroshima—Kokura bullet train in Japan which covers 120mi (192km)

in 44 minutes at an average 162.1mph (261.8km/h).

- **The TGV** from Lille to Roissy, France, covers 126mi (203km) in 48 minutes at an average speed of 158mph (254.3km/h).

- **The fastest train speed ever** was 320.2mph (515.3km/h) by the *TGV* between Courtalain and Tours, France, 1990.

- **The fastest rail speed** was 6,121mph (9,851km/h) by a rocket sled on White Sands Missile Range, New Mexico. 1982.

▼ TGV Atlantiques *often hit 184mph (300km/h) on the Eurostar from Paris to London.*

Supercars

▲ *The Porsche 911 was first introduced in 1964.*

- **The Mercedes Benz 300SL** of 1952 was one of the first supercars of the postwar years, famous for its stylish flip-up "Gullwing" doors.

- **The Jaguar E-type** was the star car of the early 1960s with sleek lines and 155mph (250km/h) performance.

- **The Ford Mustang** was one of the first young and lively "pony" cars, introduced in 1964.

- **The Aston Martin DB6** was the classic supercar of the late 1960s, driven by film spy James Bond.

- **The Porsche 911 turbo** was the fastest accelerating production car for 20 years after its launch in 1975, scorching from 0 to 60mph (100km/h) in 5.4 seconds.

- **The Lamborghini** Countach was the fastest supercar of the 1970s and 1980s, with a top speed of 183mph (295km/h).

- **The Maclaren F1** can go from 0 to 100mph (160km/h) in less time than it takes to read this sentence.

- **The Maclaren F1** can go from 0 to 100mph and back to 0 again in under 20 seconds.

- **A tuned version** of the Chevrolet Corvette, the Callaway SledgeHammer, can hit over 250mph.

> ★ **STAR FACT** ★
> The Ford GT-90 zooms from 0 to 60mph
> (100km/h) in 3.2 seconds.

A sailor's life

- **Sailors** used to be called "tars" after the tarpaulins used for making sails. Tarpaulin is canvas and tar.

- **A sailor's duties** included climbing masts, rigging sails, taking turns on watch, and swabbing (cleaning) decks.

- **The eight-hour** watches were timed with an hourglass.

- **Storing food** on ships in the days before canning was a problem. Sailors survived on biscuits and dried meat.

- **Hard tack** was hard biscuits that kept for years but often became infested with maggots. The maggots were picked out before the biscuit was eaten.

- **Every sailor** had a daily ration of a quart of water (just over a liter) since all water had to be carried on board.

- **Sailors** often made clothes from spare materials such as sail canvas.

- **Sailors who offended** against discipline might be flogged with a "cat-o'-nine-tails"—a whip with nine lengths of knotted cord.

- **Sailors slept** in any corner they could find, often next to the cannon or in the darkness below decks.

- **Sailors' lavatories** on old ships were simply holes overhanging the sea called "jardines," from the French for garden.

▼ *The introduction of the hammock in the 18th century made sleeping much less uncomfortable for sailors.*

Theaters

▶ There were several "Wooden O" theaters like this in Elizabethan London in the late 16th century, including the famous Globe, in London, England, where Shakespeare first staged his plays.

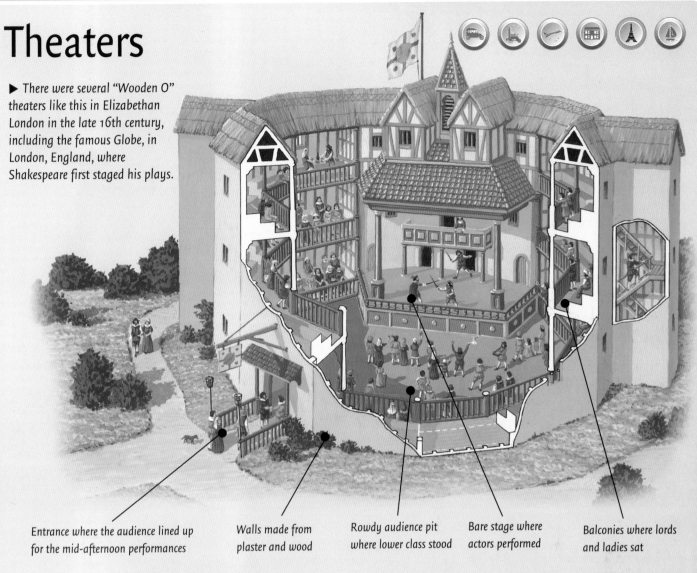

Entrance where the audience lined up for the mid-afternoon performances

Walls made from plaster and wood

Rowdy audience pit where lower class stood

Bare stage where actors performed

Balconies where lords and ladies sat

- **In the days of Ancient Greece and Rome** thousands of people went to see dramas in huge, stone-built, open-air theaters like sports arenas.

- **The Wooden Os** which appeared in England around 1570 were the first real theaters since Roman times. They were round wooden buildings with the stage and audience arena in the middle, open to the sky.

- **The 17th century** was the "Golden Age" of drama in Spain, and people crammed into open courtyard theaters called corrales to see plays by great writers, such as Caldéron de la Barca and Lope de Vega.

- **In the 17th century,** theater moved indoors for the first time. Performances were by candlelight in large halls with rows of balconies around the edge.

- **In early theaters** the actors mostly performed on a bare stage. Toward the end of the 18th century, cut-out boards with realistic scenes painted on them were slid in from the wings (the sides of the stage).

- **In the early 19th century** theaters grew much bigger to cater for the populations of the new industrial cities, often holding thousands. Huge stages were illuminated by "limelight"—brightly burning pellets of calcium.

- **Most of the grand old theaters** we can visit today date from the mid-1800s.

- **The big theaters** of the early 19th century had huge backstage areas with lots of room for "flying in" scenery, and also spring loaded trapdoors and other ingenious mechanisms for creating giant special effects, like exploding volcanoes and runaway trains.

- **Toward the end of the 19th century,** dedicated amateurs, fed up with special effects, performed in smaller spaces, such as clubs, barns, and private houses. These developed into intimate "studio" theaters where actors could stage realistic plays.

- **Many modern theaters** are equipped with very bright, computer-controlled lighting, sound systems, and motorized stage machinery.

Submarines

- **The first workable submarine** was a rowing boat covered with waterproofed skins, built by Dutch scientist Cornelius van Drebbel in 1620.

- **In 1776** David Bushnell's one-man submarine, the *Turtle*, attacked British ships in America's War of Independence.

- **Gasoline engines** and electric batteries were combined to make the first successful subs in the 1890s.

- **Powerful,** less fumy diesel engines took over from 1908.

- **In 1954** the U.S. launched the *Nautilus*, the first nuclear power sub. Now all subs are nuclear-powered.

- **U-boats** were German subs that attack Allied convoys of ships in World Wars I and II.

- **In modern sub** a strong hull of steel or titanium stops it from being crushed by the pressure of water.

> ★ **STAR FACT** ★
> The tower on the top of a submarine is called the sail or conning tower.

▶ To gain weight for a dive, submarines fill their "ballast" tanks with water. To surface, they empty the tanks.

- **Most subs** are designed for war and have long missiles called torpedoes to fire at enemy ships.

- **Attack** subs have torpedoes and guided missiles for attacking ships. Ballistic subs have missiles with nuclear warheads for firing at land targets.

Model T Ford

- **In 1905** most cars were "coach-built" which meant they were individually built by hand. This made them the costly toys of the rich only.

- **The dream of Detroit farmboy** Henry Ford was to make "a motor car for the great multitude—a car so low in price that no man making a good fortune will be unable to own one."

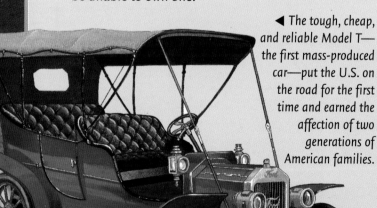

◀ The tough, cheap, and reliable Model T— the first mass-produced car—put the U.S. on the road for the first time and earned the affection of two generations of American families.

- **Ford's solution** was to make a car, which he called the Model T, by the same mass production techniques.

- **Mass production** meant using huge teams of men, each adding a small part to the car as it moved along the production line.

- **Body panels** for the Model T were stamped out by machines, not hammered by hand as with earlier cars.

- **In 1908** when Ford launched the Model T, fewer than 200,000 people in the U.S. owned cars.

- **In 1913** 250,000 people owned Model Ts alone.

- **By 1930** 15 million Model Ts had been sold.

- **One of the keys to the T** was standardizations. Ford said early Ts were available in "any color they like so long as it's black." Later models came in other colors.

- **The T's fragile-looking chassis** earned it the nickname "Tin Lizzie," but it was made of tough vanadium steel.

Bridges of wood and stone

- **The first bridges** were probably logs and vines slung across rivers to help people across.

- **The oldest known bridge** was an arch bridge built in Babylon about 2200BC.

- **Clapper bridges** are ancient bridges in which large stone slabs rest on piers (supports) of stone.

- **There are clapper bridges** in both Devon in England and Fujian in China.

- **The first brick bridges** were built by the Romans, like the Alcántara bridge over the Tagus River in Spain which was built around AD100.

- **Long bridges** could be made with a series of arches linked together. Each arch is called a span.

- **Roman arches** were semicircular, so each span was short; Chinese arches were flatter so they could span greater distances.

- **The Anji bridge** at Zhao Xian in China was built in AD610 and it is still in use today.

▲ *The Ponte Vecchio in Florence, built in 1345, is one of the oldest flattened arch bridges in Europe.*

- **Flattened arched bridges** were first built in Europe in the 14th century. Now they are the norm.

- **London Bridge** was dismantled and reconstructed stone by stone in Arizona as a tourist attraction.

Autogiros and microlights

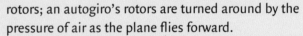

- **In the 1400s** many European children played with flying toys kept aloft by whirling blades.

- **The autogiro** was invented by the Spanish inventor Juan de la Cierva in 1923.

- **An autogiro** is lifted, not by wings, but by turning rotor blades.

- **A helicopter uses** a powerful motor to turn the rotors; an autogiro's rotors are turned around by the pressure of air as the plane flies forward.

- **The autogiro** is pulled forward by propeller blades on the front like an ordinary small plane.

- **The autogiro** can fly at up to 140mph (225km/h), but cannot hover like a helicopter.

- **In the U.S. and Australia** microlights are called ultralights. They are small, very light aircraft.

- **The first microlight** was a hang glider with a chainsaw motor, built by American hang glider pioneer Bill Bennett in 1973.

  - **Some microlights** have flexible fabric wings like hang gliders.

- **Some microlights** have fixed wings with control flaps to steer them in flight.

◄ *For a while in the 1930s, many people believed autogiros would be the Model T Fords of the air—aircraft for everyone.*

Helicopters

Without a tail rotor, the helicopter would spin around the opposite way to the main rotors. This is called torque reaction. The tail rotor also acts as a rudder to swing the tail left or right

To fly up or down, the pilot alters the angle or "pitch" of the main rotor blades with the "collective pitch" control. When the blades cut through the air almost flat, they give no lift and the helicopter sinks. To climb, the pilot steepens the pitch to increase lift

Tail rotor drive shaft

To fly forward or back, or for a banked turn, the pilot tilts the whole rotor with the "cyclic pitch" control

The angle of the blades is changed via rods linked to a sliding collar round the rotor shaft, called the swashplate

Rockets

Engine

Stabilizers

▶ A helicopter's rotor blades are long, thin wings. The engine whirls them around so that they cut through the air and provide lift just like conventional wings (see Taking off). But they are also like huge propellers, hauling the helicopter up just as a propeller pulls a plane.

● **Toy helicopters** have been around for centuries, and those made by air pioneer Sir George Cayley in the early 19th century are the most famous.

● **On November 13, 1907** a primitive helicopter with two sets of rotors lifted French mechanic Paul Cornu off the ground for 20 seconds.

● **The problem** with pioneer helicopters was control. The key was to vary the pitch of the rotor blades.

● **In 1937** German designer Heinrich Focke built an aircraft with two huge variable pitch rotors instead of wings and achieved a controlled hover. Months later, German Anton Flettner built the first true helicopter.

● **Focke and Flettner's** machines had two rotors turning in opposite directions to prevent torque reaction. In 1939, Russian born American Igor Sikorsky solved the problem by adding a tail rotor.

● **The Jesus nut** that holds the main rotor to the shaft got its name because pilots said, "Oh Jesus, if that nut comes off...."

● **The biggest helicopter** was the Russian Mil Mi-12 Homer of 1968 which could lift 44 tons (40,204kg) up to 7,400ft (2,255m).

● **The fastest helicopter** is the Westland Lynx, which flew at 250mph (402km/h) on August 6, 1986.

● **The Boeing/Sikorsky RAH-66** Comanche unveiled in 1999 is the first helicopter using stealth technology (see warplanes).

▲ The Vietnam war saw the rise of heavily armed helicopter gunships designed to hit targets such as tanks.

! NEWS FLASH !
The Bell Quad Tiltrotor has wings like a plane for fast flying. The propellers on the end of each wing tilt up in 20 seconds for vertical lift off. It could evacuate 100 people from danger in minutes.

Dams

▲ The gates of the Thames Barrier in London are designed to shut in times of very high tides to stop seawater flooding the city.

- **The earliest known dam** is a 50ft (15m) high brick dam on the Nile River at Kosheish, Egypt, built around 2900BC.

- **Two Ancient Roman** brick dams, at Proserpina and Cornalbo in southwest Spain, are still in use today.

- **In China** a stone dam was built on the Gukow in 240BC.

- **Masonry dams** today are usually built of concrete blocks as gravity dams, arch dams, or buttress dams.

- **Gravity dams** are very thick dams relying entirely on a huge weight of concrete to hold the water.

- **Arch dams** are built in narrow canyons and curve upstream. Buttress dams are thin dams strengthened by supports called buttresses on the downstream side.

- **Embankment dams** or fill dams are simple dams built from piles of soil, stones, gravel, or clay.

- **The Aswan dam** on the Nile in Egypt has created Lake Nasser—one of the world's biggest artificial lakes.

- **The world's highest dams** are fill dams in Tajikistan: the Rogun, 1,100ft (335m) and Nurek, 985ft (300m). The highest gravity dam is the 935ft (285m) Grand Dixence in Switzerland. The highest arch dam is the 892ft (272m) Inguri in Georgia.

> ★ **STAR FACT** ★
> The world's biggest dam is the 837ft (255m) high Kambaratinsk Dam in Russia.

Warships

- **21st-century navies** have five main classes of surface warship in descending size order: aircraft carriers, assault ships, cruisers, destroyers, and frigates.

- **The biggest** warships are 1,092ft (333m) long U.S. aircraft carriers Nimitz, Dwight D. Eisenhower, Carl Vinson, Abraham Lincoln, John C. Stennis, George Washington, and Harry S Truman.

- **In World War II** cruisers had big guns; destroyers protected the main fleet; and frigates protected slower ships against submarines.

- **The distinction between** classes is now blurred. Many small warships carry helicopters or even VTOL planes (see Warplanes).

▶ A 1940s destroyer armed with a rotating gun for fleet escort.

- **The Russian** Moskva class are a cross between cruisers and aircraft carriers with rear flight decks for helicopters.

- **The British** Invincible class are small aircraft carriers able to carry six Harrier jump jets and twelve helicopters.

- **Warships** have largely replaced guns with guided missiles.

- **Warships** have both short-range missiles to fire against missiles and long-range supersonic missiles to fire against ships.

- **The U.S. Ticonderoga** ships are small cruisers built in the 1970s. They are powered by gas-turbine engines and armed with Tomahawk missiles.

- **The nuclear-powered** Russian Kirov class begun in 1973 are among the few big cruisers, over 22,000 tons.

Steam locomotives

- **Steam locomotives** get their power by burning coal in a firebox. This heats up water in a boiler, making steam. The steam drives a piston and the piston turns the wheels via connecting rods and cranks.

- **It takes about three hours** for the crew to get up enough steam to get a locomotive moving.

- **Coal and water** are often stored in a wagon called a tender, towed behind the locomotive.

- **A tender** holds 10 tons of coal and 8,000gal (30,000l) of water.

- **Locomotive classes** are described by their wheel layout.

- **A 4-6-2** has four small leading "bogie" wheels, six big driving wheels and two small trailing wheels. The small bogie wheels carry much of the weight.

> ★ STAR FACT ★
> The first locomotive to hit 100mph (160km/h) was the *City of Truro* in 1895.

- **The greatest Victorian** locomotive designer was James Nasmyth.

- **In the American Civil War** (1861–65) the locomotive *The General* was recaptured by Confederates.

- *The Flying Scotsman* was a famous locomotive designed by Sir Nigel Gresley (1876–1941). It pulled trains 380mi (663km) from London to Edinburgh in under six hours.

▼ An American locomotive of the 1890s.

Dhows

- **Dhows** are wooden Arab boats that have been used in the waters of the Mediterranean and Indian Ocean for thousands of years.

- **Most dhows** are now made of teak (or Glass Reinforced Plastic). In the past, mango wood was common.

▼ Dhows like this are still built today in Lamu in Africa, much as they were 1,000 or more years ago.

- **In the past** dhows were made, not by nailing planks of wood together, but by sewing them with coconut fiber.

- **Dhow builders** rarely work from plans. They judge entirely by eye and experience.

- **Dhows traditionally** had lateen sails—triangular sails in line with the boat. This lets them sail into the wind.

- **Although many dhows** are now motorized, they usually have a tall mast for unloading.

- **There are several kinds** of dhow, including the shu'ai, the boum, the sambuq, the jelbut, and the ghanjah.

- **The jelbut** is thought to get its name from the English "jolly boat"—the little boats visiting British East Indiamen. Jelbuts were often used for pearl fishing. Racing jelbuts have a tree trunk-like bowsprit almost as long as the hull to carry extra sails.

- **Sambuqs and ghanjahs** are thought to get their square sterns from 17th century Portuguese galleons.

- **Boums** can be up to 400 tons and 165ft (50m) long.

Towns and cities

▲ The city of Florence is one of the most beautiful in the world. Many buildings date from the time when European towns began to flourish in the 15th century—especially in Italy.

- **The first cities** may date from the time when hunters and gatherers settled down to farm 10,000 years ago.

- **The city of Jericho** has been settled for over 10,000 years.

- **One of the oldest** known cities is Catal Hüyük in Anatolia in Turkey, dating from earlier than 6000BC.

- **The first Chinese cities** developed around 1600BC.

- **The cities of Ancient Greece** and Rome were often carefully laid out, with major public buildings. The first known town planner was the Ancient Greek Hippodamus, who planned the city of Miletus.

- **In the 1200s** Paris was by far the biggest city in Europe with a population of 150,000.

- **In the 1200s** 320,000 people lived in Hangzhou in China; Guangzhou (Canton) was home to 250,000.

- **In the 1400s** towns like Genoa, Bruges, and Antwerp grew as trading centers. Medieval towns were rarely planned.

- **In the 1800s** huge industrial cities based on factories grew rapidly. Chicago's population jumped from 4,000 in 1840 to 1 million in 1890.

- **The fastest growing** cities are places like Sao Paulo in Brazil where many poor people live in quickly erected shanty towns. The world's biggest city is Mexico City.

Luxury cars

- **The first Rolls-Royce** was made by Charles Rolls and Henry Royce. It was known as the "best car in the world."

- **The Rolls-Royce Silver Ghost** got its name for its ghost-like quietness and shiny aluminum body.

- **Today** each Rolls-Royce takes three months to build.

- **The winged girl** statuette on the hood of a Rolls-Royce is called "Spirit of Ecstasy" and dates from 1911.

- **In the 1930s** Ettore Bugatti set out to build the best car ever with the Bugatti Royale. Only six were built, and they are now the world's most valuable cars.

- **The name Royale** comes from the King of Spain, Alfonso XIII, who was to buy the first model.

- **In 1925** drinksmaker André Dubonnet had a special version of the Hispano-Suiza H6B built with a body made entirely of tulipwood.

- **In the 1930s** American carmakers like Cord, Auburn, and Packard made magnificent cars that Hollywood stars posed beside and Chicago gangsters drove.

- **Every 1934** Auburn speedster was sold with a plaque certifying it had been driven at over 100mph (160km/h) by racing driver Ab Jenkins.

- **The Mercedes in** Mercedes-Benz was the name of the daughter of Emil Jellinek, who sold the cars in the U.S.

▶ Bentley is one of the great names in luxury cars. But founder Owen Bentley believed in racing as advertisement. The Bentley name gained lasting fame with success in the Le Mans 24-hour races of the 1920s. Seen here is a 1950s rally entry.

Towers

- **Romans, Byzantines,** and medieval Europeans built defensive towers in city walls and by gates to give platforms for raining missiles on enemies.

- **Early churches** had square towers as landmarks to be seen from afar. From the 1100s, European cathedrals had towers called steeples, topped by a pointed spire.

- **Spires began** as pyramids on a tower, but were tapered to make a steeple.

- **In the 17th and 18th centuries** church spires became simple and elegant, as in Park Street Church, Boston.

- **The tallest unsupported tower** is Toronto's 1,815ft (553m) high CN tower.

- **The tallest** tower supported by cables is the 2,065ft (629m) TV broadcast tower near Fargo and Blanchard.

- **The Tower of Babel** was a legendary tower built in ancient Babylon in the Near East. The Bible says God didn't want this high tower built, so he made the builders speak different languages to confuse them.

- **The Pharos** was a 443ft (135m) lighthouse built around 283BC to guide ships into the harbor at Alexandria in Egypt.

- **The Tower of Winds,** or Horologium, was built in Athens around 100BC to hold a sundial, weather vane, and water clock.

- **Big Ben** is the clock in St. Stephen's Tower in London's Houses of Parliament. The tower had a cell where "rioters" like suffragette Emmeline Pankhurst were held.

◄ *The Leaning Tower of Pisa in Italy is a 180ft (55m) high belltower or campanile. Building began in 1173. It started to lean as workers built the third story. It is now 14.5ft (4.4m) out of true.*

The first houses

- **It was once thought** prehistoric humans lived in caves, but caves were for religious rituals. The earliest houses were made of perishable materials like wood, leaves, grass, and mud—so all traces have long since vanished.

- **Stone Age people** probably lived in round huts, with walls of wooden posts and thatches of reed.

- **In Britain** post holes and hearths have been found dating back 10,000 years in places like London's Hampstead Heath and Broom Hill in Hampshire.

- **Early mudbrick** houses dating from at least 9,500 years ago are found in Anatolia in the Middle East.

- **Low walls** of stones were the base for thatched roofs 6,500 years ago at places like Carn Brea in Cornwall, England.

- **Two-story houses** in Mohenjo Daro in Pakistan from 5,000 years ago were built from sun-dried mud bricks and had courtyards, doors, windows, and bathrooms.

- **Big Ancient Egyptian** houses had three main areas—a reception room for business, a hall in the center for guests, and private quarters at the back for family members.

- **Tomb models** show what Egyptian homes were like.

- **Big Roman country houses** were called villas; a town house was called a domus.

- **Villas** had tiled roofs, verandahs, marbled floors, lavishly decorated walls, bathrooms, and even heating.

◄ *Some home-building styles have changed little in thousands of years. These stilt houses are in French Polynesia.*

Record-breaking cars

★ **STAR FACT** ★

On October 13, 1997, a British jet car called *Thrust SSC* driven by British fighter pilot Andy Green broke the sound barrier for the first time. In two runs across Nevada's Black Rock desert it hit over 760mph (1,220km/h).

- **The first car speed record** was achieved by an electric Jentaud car in 1898 at Acheres near Paris. Driven by the Comte de Chasseloup-Laubat, the car hit 39.24mph (63.14km/h). Camille Jenatzy vied with de Chasseloup-Laubat for the record, raising it to 65.79mph (105.88km/h) in his car *Jamais Contente* in 1899.

- **Daytona Beach** in Florida became a venue for speed trials in 1903.

- **The biggest engine** ever to be raced in a Grand Prix was the 19,891 cc V4 of American Walter Christie, which he entered in the 1907 French Grand Prix. Later the Christie was the first front-wheel drive car to win a major race—a 250mi (400km) race on Daytona Beach.

- **The record** for the outer circuit at Brooklands, England was set in 1935 by John Cobb in a Napier-Railton at 1 min 0.41 sec, 143.44mph (230.84km/h) and never beaten.

- **In 1911** the governing body for the land speed record said that cars had to make two runs in opposite directions over a 0.6mi (1km) course to get the record.

- **In 1924** Sir Malcolm Campbell broke the Land Speed Record for the first of many times in a Sunbeam at 146.16mph (235.22km/h). In 1925 he hit 150mph (242 km/h) for the first time. But his most famous record-breaking runs were in the 1930s in his own *Bluebirds*.

- **In 1947** John Cobb drove with tremendous skill to reach 394.20mph (634.39km/h) in his Railton-Mobil. This stood as the record for 17 years.

- **In 1964** the rules were changed to allow jet and rocket-propelled cars to challenge for the Land Speed Record. The next year Craig Breedlove drove his three-wheeler jet *Spirit of America* to over 500mph (800km/h).

- **In 1970** Gary Gabelich set the record over 622mph (1,000km/h) in his rocket-powered *Blue Flame*. This record wasn't beaten until Richard Noble roared to 633.47mph (1,019.44km/h) in his Rolls-Royce jet-powered *Thrust 2* in 1983.

▼ Donald Campbell took on the record-breaking mantle of his father—and the Bluebird name for his car. On July 17, 1964, Campbell's Bluebird hit a world record 403.10mph (648.71km/h) on the salt flats at Lake Eyre in South Australia.

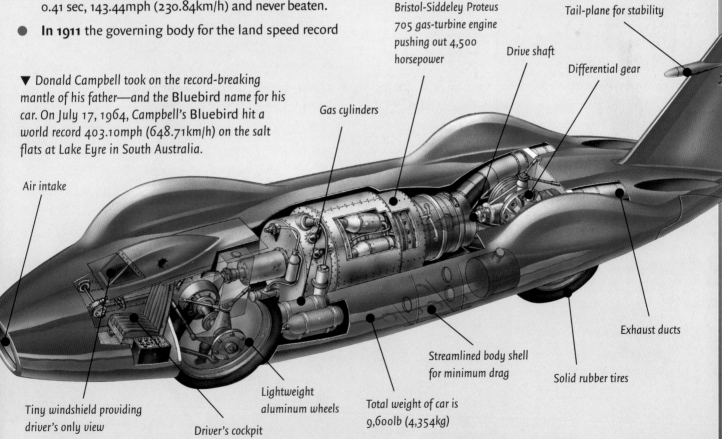

Bristol-Siddeley Proteus 705 gas-turbine engine pushing out 4,500 horsepower

Tail-plane for stability

Drive shaft

Differential gear

Gas cylinders

Air intake

Exhaust ducts

Streamlined body shell for minimum drag

Solid rubber tires

Tiny windshield providing driver's only view

Lightweight aluminum wheels

Driver's cockpit

Total weight of car is 9,600lb (4,354kg)

Ocean liners

▲ One of the great transatlantic liners of the 1930s, the Queen Mary (sistership of the Queen Elizabeth) is now a hotel at Long Beach California.

- **The great age** of ocean liners lasted from the early 1900s to the 1950s.

- **Ocean liners** were huge boats, often with luxurious cabins, bars, games rooms, and swimming pools.

- **The main route** was across the Atlantic. From 1833 liners competed for the Blue Riband title for fastest crossing.

- **Great Blue Riband** contenders included Brunel's *Great Western* in the 1830s, the *Mauretania* which held it from 1907 to 1929, and the French *Normandie* of the 1930s.

- **The last** ocean liner to hold the Blue Riband was the *United States* in the 1960s.

- **The famous Cunard line** was set up by Nova Scotia Quaker Samuel Cunard with George Burns and David MacIver in 1839.

- **The *Titanic* of 1912** was the largest ship ever built at 46,329 tons when launched in 1912—but it sank on its maiden (first) voyage.

- **The sinking** of the liner *Lusitania* by a German submarine on May 7, 1915 with the loss of 1,198 lives spurred the U.S. to join the war against Germany.

- **The *Queen Elizabeth*,** launched in 1938, was the largest passenger ship ever built—1,030ft (314m) long and 83,673 tons. It sank during refitting in Hong Kong, 1972.

- **Future liners** may be based on FastShip technology, with a very broad flat hull for high-speed stability.

The Tower of London

- **The Tower of London** is the oldest stone castle in London, started by William the Conqueror after his conquest of England in 1066. The Crown Jewels are kept here.

- **The oldest part of the tower** is the great square keep called the White Tower which dates from 1078.

- **The Tower** later gained two surrounding "curtain" walls, like other castles.

- **The inner curtain** wall has 13 towers, including the Bloody Tower, Beauchamp Tower, and Wakefield Tower.

- **Traitors' Gate** is an arch beside the River Thames. High-ranking traitors were brought this way by boat to be imprisoned in the Tower.

▶ The Tower of London is the most famous medieval castle in Britain.

- **Many people** have been imprisoned here, like Princess (later Queen) Elizabeth and her mother Anne Boleyn in the 1500s.

- **Little Ease** is a dark 35 sq ft (3.3 sq m) cell where prisoners could neither stand up nor lie down.

- **Many prisoners were** beheaded here, such as Sir Thomas More and Sir Walter Raleigh.

- **In 1483** the boy king Edward V and his young brother were thought to have been murdered here. Bones which could have been theirs were later found.

- **Yeoman Warders** are the Tower's special guards. They are nicknamed beefeaters. The name may come from a fondness for roast beef or the French word *buffetier*.

Greek and Roman building

▲ ▶ *The most famous Greek temple is the Parthenon in Athens, built c.450 BC.*

- **Ancient Greek and Roman** architecture are together known as Classical architecture.

- **The key features** of Classical buildings are solid, elegantly plain geometric shapes including pillars, arches, and friezes.

- **The main Greek** building was the temple with its triangular roof of pale stone on rows of tall columns.

- **Greek temples** were designed in mathematical ratios.

- **Roman architect** Vitruvius described three orders (styles) of columns: Doric, Ionic, and Corinthian.

- **Each order** has its own character: Doric serious and strong, Ionic graceful, and Corinthian rich and festive.

- **The Parthenon** is a Doric temple built by architects Ictinus and Callicrates guided by the sculptor Phidias.

- **Roman buildings** used many arches and vaults (ceilings made from arches joined together).

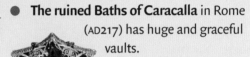

- **The ruined Baths of Caracalla** in Rome (AD217) has huge and graceful vaults.

- **Classical** architecture has inspired many imitations over the centuries, including the Palladian style of the 1600s.

Peoples' cars

- **The first car** for ordinary people was Ford's Model T. Ford built their ten millionth car in 1924 and their 50 millionth in 1959.

- **The U.S.** began making more than one million cars a year in 1916, of which over a third were Model Ts. No other country made a million cars a year until the U.K. in 1954.

- **Ford U.S.** introduced weekly installment plans for new cars in 1923. The Nazis later borrowed the idea for the VW Beetle.

- **The Model A Ford** sold one million within 14 months of its launch in December 1927. The Ford Escort of 1980 sold a million in just 11 months.

- **The French Citroën 2CV** was designed to carry "a farmer in a top hat across a plowed field without breaking the eggs on the seat beside him."

- **The VW Beetle** was the brain child of the Nazi dictator Adolf Hitler who wanted a cheap car for all Germans. It was created in 1938 by Ferdinand Porsche.

- **The war interrupted** VW Beetle production before it had barely begun, but it was resumed after the war.

- **The ten millionth** VW Beetle was built in 1965. Over 22 million have now been sold.

- **The Soviet built Lada,** based on a design by Fiat, was one of the cheapest cars ever.

- **The first British car** to sell a million was the Morris Minor, between 1949 and 1962.

▼ *The 1959 Mini, designed by Alec Issigonis, set a trend in small car design.*

Bridges

▲ London's Tower Bridge was opened in 1894. It has a strong steel frame clothed in stone to support the two opening halves.

- **Rope suspension** bridges have been used for thousands of years. One of the first to use iron chains was the Lan Jin Bridge at Yunnan in China, built AD65.

- **The first** all-iron bridge was at Coalbrookdale, England. It was designed by Thomas Pritchard and built in 1779 by Abraham Darby.

- **In the early 1800s** Thomas Telford began building superb iron bridges such as Craigellachie over the Spey in Scotland (1814). He built Europe's first iron chain suspension bridge over the Menai Straits in Wales in 1826.

- **Stephenson's** Britannia railway bridge of 1850, also over the Menai Straits, was the first hollow box girder bridge.

▶ Most bridges are now built of concrete and steel. Shown here are some of the main kinds. The longest are normally suspension bridges, usually carrying roads, but Hong Kong's 4,518ft (1,377m) long Tsing Ma (1998) takes both road and rail.

★ **STAR FACT** ★
The Akashi-Kaikyo Bridge, Japan, is the world's longest suspension bridge, with a main span of 6,532ft (1,991m).

- **John Roebling's** Cincinnati suspension bridge was the world's longest bridge when built in 1866 at 1,056ft (322m). Like all suspension bridges today, it was held up by iron wires, not chains. It was the prototype for his Brooklyn Bridge.

- **The Forth Railway Bridge** in Scotland was the world's first big cantilevered bridge.

- **In 1940** the Tacoma suspension bridge in Washington State was blown down by a moderate wind just months after its completion. The disaster forced engineers to make suspension bridges aerodynamic.

- **Aerodynamic design** played a major part in the design of Turkey's Bosphorus Bridge (1973) and England's Humber Bridge (1983).

- **In the 1970s** Japanese engineers began to build a kind of steel bridge which meant that by 2000, Japan had nine of the world's 20 longest bridges.

In suspension bridges the bridge hangs on steel wires on a cable suspended between tall towers. They are light so can be very long

In cable-stayed bridges, the bridge hangs directly from steel cables

In cantilevered bridges, each half of the bridge is balanced on a support

Arch bridges are one of the oldest kinds and make very strong bridges

Bascule or lifting bridges like London's Tower Bridge swing up in the middle to allow tall ships through

Steel or concrete beam bridges are carried on piers. The beam may be a hollow steel girder through which cars and trains can run

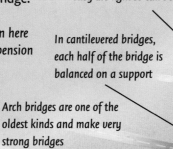

The Statue of Liberty

- **New York's Statue of Liberty** stands on Liberty Island off the tip of Manhattan.

- **The statue** was dedicated on Oct 28, 1886 by President Cleveland.

- **It was paid** for by the French people to celebrate their friendship with the United States.

- **Sculptor** Frédéric-Auguste Bartholdi began work on the statue in Paris in 1875.

◀ *New York's Statue of Liberty, before it was restored in 1986 and the flame covered in gold leaf.*

- **It was built** from 452 copper sheets hammered into shape by hand and mounted on four huge steel supports designed by Eiffel and Viollet-le-Duc.

- **The 225-ton statue** was shipped to New York in 1885.

- **A pedestal** designed by Richard Hunt and paid for by 121,000 Americans brought it to a height of 305ft (93m).

- **The statue's** full name is *Liberty Enlightening the World*. The seven spikes in the crown stand for Liberty's light shining on the world's seven seas and continents. The tablet in Her left hand is America's Declaration of Independence.

- **Emma Lazarus's sonnet** *The New Colossus* on the pedestal ends: "Give me your tired poor, your huddled masses of your teeming shore. Send these, the homeless, tempest-tossed to me. I lift my lamp beside the golden door!"

★ STAR FACT ★
Every year, two million people visit the Statue of Liberty.

Buses and coaches

- **Horse-drawn stage coaches** were the first regular public coach services between two or more points or "stages." They were first used in London in the 1630s.

- **Stage coaches** reached their heyday in the early 1800s when new tarred roads made travel faster. Coaches went from London to Edinburgh in 40 hours.

- **Bus is short** for "omnibus," meaning "for all" in Latin. The word first came into use in Paris in the 1820s for big coaches carrying lots of people on local trips

- **In 1830** Goldsworthy Gurney put a steam engine in a coach to make the first powered bus. It ran four times a day between Cheltenham and Gloucester in England.

- **In the 1850s** British government laws restricted steam road vehicles, so big new cities developed horse buses.

- **In 1895** a gasoline-engine bus was built in Germany.

- **In 1904** the London General Omnibus Co. ran the first gasoline-engine bus services.

- **1905:** the first motor buses ran on New York's 5th Avenue.

▲ *Like most early buses, this one from the early 1920s was built by adding a coach body to a truck base.*

- **In 1928** the first transcontinental bus service crossed the United States.

- **From the 1950s** trailer buses were used in European cities. A trailer joined to the bus carries extra passengers.

St. Basil's Cathedral

- **The cathedral of** St. Basil the Blessed in Moscow's Red Square was built from 1554 to 1560.

- **St. Basil's** is made up of ten tower churches: the biggest is 150ft (46m) tall.

- **It began with** eight little wooden churches, each built between 1552 and 1554 after a major Russian victory against the Tartars of Kazan.

- **After the final victory**, Ivan the Terrible ordered stone churches to be built in place of the wooden ones.

- **Legend says** each of the onion-shaped domes represents the turban of a defeated Tartar lord.

▲ With its ten famous colorful towers, St. Basil's in Moscow is like no other Christian cathedral in the world.

- **St. Basil's** may have been designed by two Russians: Posnik and Barma.

- **Legend says** the Italian builder was blinded afterward so he could build nothing like it again.

- **Originally** it was known as the Cathedral of the Intercession, but in 1588 a tenth church was added in honor of St. Basil. It was known afterward as St. Basil's.

- **Napoleon and Stalin** both tried to destroy the cathedral.

- **In 1955**, restorers found the secret of the cathedral's construction embedded in the brickwork—wooden models used as silhouettes to guide the builders.

Hydrofoils

- **Hydrofoils** are boats with hulls that lift up above the water when traveling at high speeds.

- **The hydrofoils** are wings attached to the hull by struts that move underwater like airplane wings and lift the boat up.

- **Because only the foils** dip in the water, hydrofoils avoid water resistance, so can travel faster with less power.

- **Surface-piercing hydrofoils** are used in calm inland waters and skim across the surface.

▼ By lifting themselves out of the water and almost flying across the surface, hydrofoils achieve very high speeds.

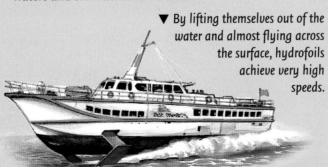

★ STAR FACT ★
The biggest hydrofoil is the 210ft (64m) long, 57mph (92km/h) *Plainview* navy ship.

- **Full-submerged hydrofoils** dip deep into the water for stability in seagoing boats.

- **The foils** are usually in two sets: bow and stern.

- **The bow and stern foils** are in one of three arrangements. "Canard" means the stern foil is bigger. "Airplane" means the bow foil is bigger. "Tandem" means they are both the same size.

- **The first successful hydrofoil** was built by Italian Enrico Forlanini in 1906.

- **In 1918** Alexander Graham Bell, inventor of the telephone, built a hydrofoil that set a world water speed record at 61.6 knots (70.8mph/114km/h). The record was not beaten until the American *Fresh 1*, another hydrofoil, set a new record of 84 knots (96.6mph/155km/h) in 1963.

Balloons

- **Balloons** are bags filled with a light gas or hot air—both so light that the balloon floats in the air.

- **Balloons** designed to carry people into the air are of two types: hot-air balloons and gas balloons filled with hydrogen or helium.

- **Hot-air balloons** have a burner that continually fills the balloon with warm air to keep it afloat.

- **To carry two people** a hot-air balloon must have a bag of about 2,225 cu yd (1,700 cu m) in volume.

- **Balloons** are normally launched at dusk or dawn when the air is quite calm.

- **As the air in the bag cools**, the balloon gradually sinks. To maintain height, the balloonist lights the burner to add warm air again.

- **To descend quickly** the balloonist pulls a cord to let air out through a vent in the top of the bag.

- **The first flight** in a hot-air balloon was made in Paris on October 15, 1783 by French scientist Jean de Rozier in a

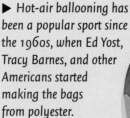 ▶ Hot-air ballooning has been a popular sport since the 1960s, when Ed Yost, Tracy Barnes, and other Americans started making the bags from polyester.

balloon made by the Montgolfier brothers.

- **The first hydrogen gas balloon flight** was on December 1, 1783 in Paris by Jacques Charles and one of the two Robert brothers.

- **On March 20, 1999** Swiss Bertran Piccard and British Brian Jones made the first round-the-world hot-air balloon flight.

Record-breaking flights

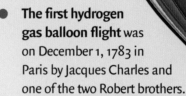

- **On July 25, 1909** Louis Blériot made the first flight across the English Channel in a plane he built himself.

- **On May 8–31, 1919** Capt. A.C. Read and his crew made the first flight across the Atlantic in a Curtiss flying boat.

- **On June 14–15, 1919** John Alcock and Arthur Brown made the first nonstop flight across the Atlantic in an open cockpit Vickers Vimy biplane.

★ STAR FACT ★
In December 1986, the American plane *Voyager*, piloted by Dick Rutan and Jeana Yeager, flew around the world non-stop in nine days .

- **On November 12–December 10, 1921** Keith and Ross Smith made the first flight from England to Australia.

- **In February 1921** William Corey was the first person to fly solo across the United States.

- **In 1927** Frenchman Louis Breguet made the first flight across the South Atlantic.

- **On May 21, 1927** American Charles Lindbergh made the first solo flight across the Atlantic in the *Spirit of St Louis*.

- **In July 1931** Wiley Post made the fastest round-the-world flight yet.

- **The story of Post's epic** flight was told in the book *Round the World in Eight Days*.

◀ Louis Blériot's first flight across the English Channel in 1909.

St. Paul's Cathedral

- **The current St. Paul's** Cathedral in London is the fifth church on the site.

- **On the same site** in Roman times, there was a temple dedicated to Diana.

- **The first St. Paul's** was built of wood in AD604 by St. Ethelbert, King of Kent.

- **The Norman cathedral** was started around 1090 by Maurice, chaplain to William the Conqueror.

- **The Norman cathedral** called "Old St. Paul's" had the highest spire ever built, but it was struck down by lightning in 1561.

- **The first public lottery** was held in Old St. Paul's in 1569 to raise money for repairs. The churchyard was famous for its booksellers, like Wynkyn de Worde in the 1400s.

◄ St. Paul's is one of the world's largest cathedrals. It was built in the classical (Roman) style by the great architect Christopher Wren in the 17th century.

- **Old St. Paul's** burned to the ground in the Great Fire of London in 1666.

- **The new St. Paul's** was designed by Sir Christopher Wren, who designed many other London buildings. Wren thought the 365ft (111m) high dome he wanted to be seen from the outside was too lofty for the inside. So inside the outer dome, he built another 65ft (20m) lower. Work began in 1675 and was completed in 1711.

- **If you whisper** inside the dome's "whispering gallery" you can be heard on the far side 115ft (35m) away.

- **Among the famous tombs** in the crypt of St. Paul's are those of Admiral Nelson and the Duke of Wellington.

Boat building

◄ Building boats in wood is a tremendously skilled craft that dates back many thousands of years.

- **For much of history** ships were built and designed by shipwrights.

- **Shipwrights** worked from experience and rarely drew plans. But in the 17th and 18th centuries, they often made models.

- **Nowadays** ships are designed by "naval architects" and built by shipbuilders.

> **★ STAR FACT ★**
> A futtock is one of the big bent timber ribs of a boat near the stern.

- **Wooden ships** were put together on a building berth. Timbers and planks were cut and shaped around, then fitted together on the berth to form the ship's hull.

- **First the long spine** or keel of the boat was laid down. Thick wooden ribs were added to make a strong frame.

- **In the Middle Ages** in the Mediterranean, wooden ships were carvel-built. This means the planks were fitted together edge to edge onto the ribs.

- **In the Middle Ages** in northern Europe, wooden ships were clinker-built. This means the planks overlapped, as in Viking ships.

- **Ships** are launched down a slope called a slipway.

- **After launching** a ship has just the bare bones of a hull and main structures. It is finished in a fitting-out basin.

Hovercraft

- **A hovercraft** or air cushion vehicle floats on a layer of compressed air just above the ground. It is also called a ground-effect machine. The air means there is very little friction between the craft and the ground.

- **A hovercraft** has one or more big fans that suck air into the craft, then blow it down underneath. The air is trapped underneath by a flexible rubber skirt.

- **The idea began with** Sir John Thornycroft in the 1870s. He thought drag on a ship's hull could be reduced if an indent in the hull allowed it to ride on a cushion of air. But for decades no one could figure out how to contain the air.

- **In the 1950s** Christopher Cockerell cracked the problem by pumping air down around the edge of a curtain-like skirt. The air itself then sealed the cushion of air inside the curtain.

- **In 1959** the world's first practical hovercraft, the SRN1 was built, using Cockerell's system. It crossed the English Channel on the 50th anniversary of Blériot's first flight across the Channel.

- **In the late 1960s** the U.S. Army and navy began using hovercraft in the Vietnam war for patrol and rescue missions because of their ability to go over land, water, and swampy ground equally easily. The Russian and U.S. armies are still the biggest users of hovercraft.

- **In 1968** big hovercraft able to carry scores of cars and trucks were introduced as ferries across the English Channel, but elsewhere they have not lived up to expectations. The biggest cross-Channel hovercraft was the 185ft (56m) long SRN4 MkIII which carried 418 passengers and 60 cars.

- **In the late 1950s** French engineer Jean Bertin developed a train called a tracked air cushion vehicle or TACV. This is like a hovercraft on rails. Trains like this could swish between cities almost silently at speeds of 300mph (500km/h).

- **On January 25, 1980** a 100 ton U.S. Navy hovercraft, the SES 100-B, reached a record speed of 105.6mph (170km/h)—faster than any warship has ever traveled.

> **! NEWS FLASH !**
> Hospitals can use special hoverbeds to support badly burned patients on air.

▼ Hovercraft vary in speed, size, and power, but they are used essentially for one of two purposes: as ferries across short stretches of water, like this one, or by the army and navy.

Rubberized bag skirt, holding the air cushion in

Flight deck

Powerful gas turbine for the lifting fan

Passenger compartment in which people travel as they would on an airplane. There is no deck as on a conventional boat

Double propellers for driving the hovercraft forward or backward at speeds of up to 72mph (120km/h)

Rudders to steer the craft. These become more effective the faster the hovercraft is traveling

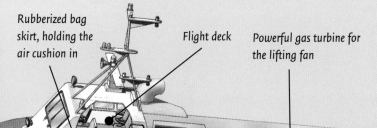

Chinese building

- **China** developed its own distinctive style of building over 3,000 years ago.
- **Traditionally, large Chinese buildings** were made of wood on a stone base.
- **A distinctive feature** is a large tiled overhanging roof, ending in a graceful upturn. The tiles were glazed blue, green, or yellow.
- **The roof** is supported not by the walls but by wooden columns, often carved and painted red and gold.
- **Walls were thin** and simply gave privacy and warmth.
- **Chinese temples** were large wooden halls with elaborate roof beams in the ceiling.
- **Pagodas** are tall tapering towers often linked to Buddhist temples. They have from 3 to 15 stories.

> ★ STAR FACT ★
> Chinese pagodas have eight sides and an uneven number of stories.

▲ The Forbidden City in Beijing dates mostly from the Ming era from 1368–1644. Only the emperor's household could enter it.

- **In China, pagodas** were believed to bring happiness to the surrounding community. They were made of wood, bricks, tiles, or even porcelain and decorated with ivory.
- **Pagodas** came from India and developed from Buddhist burial mounds called stupas.

Canoes

- **The first canoes** were scooped out logs.
- **A skin canoe** was made by stretching animal skins over a bent wood frame.
- **A skin canoe** dating from around 4500BC was found on the Baltic island of Fünen.

◀ ▼ The materials may be different, but today's bright fiberglass canoes (left) are based on the same principles as the ancient bark canoes of Native Americans (below).

- **Some skin canoes** are round like the Indian paracil and the Welsh coracle.
- **Some skin canoes** are long and thin like the Irish curach and the Inuit kayak.
- **Kayaks** have a watertight cover made from sealskin to keep out water in rough conditions.
- **The ancient quffa** of Iraq is a large canoe made of basketwork sealed with tar and dates back to 4000BC.
- **Native Americans** made canoes from bark. The Algonquins used paper birch, the Iroquois elm.
- **Bark canoes** were the basis for today's sport canoes of fiberglass, plastic, and aluminum.
- **Unlike ordinary boats,** canoes are often so light that they can easily be carried overland to avoid waterfalls or to move from one river to another.

Electric trains

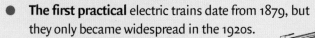

- **The first practical** electric trains date from 1879, but they only became widespread in the 1920s.

- **Electric locomotives** pick up electric current either from a third "live" rail or from overhead cables.

- **To pick up** power from overhead cables, locomotives need a spring-loaded frame or pantograph to keep in contact.

- **Electric trains** are clean and powerful, and are also able to travel faster than other trains.

- **Older systems** mostly used Direct Current (DC) motors, operating at 1,500–3,000 volts for overhead cables and 700 volts for live rails.

- **High-speed trains** like France's *TGV* and Japan's *Shinkansen* use "three-phase" Alternating Current (AC) motors operating at 25,000 volts.

◀ *Japan's Shinkansen "bullet train" was the first of the modern high-speed electric trains, regularly operating at speeds of over 250mph (400km/h).*

- **The Paris–London** *Eurostar* works on 25,000 volt AC overhead cables in France, and 750 volt live rails after it comes out of the Channel Tunnel in England.

- **Magnetic levitation** or maglev trains do not have wheels but glide along supported by electromagnets.

- **In electrodynamic maglevs**, the train rides on repulsing magnets. In electromagnetic maglevs, they hang from attracting magnets.

- **Maglevs** are used now only for short, low-speed trains, but they may one day be the fastest of all. High-speed maglev developments now use "superconducting" electromagnets which are costly to make. But a new idea is to use long strings of ordinary permanent magnets.

Stations

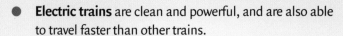

- **London Bridge** station is the oldest big city terminal, first built from wood in 1836, then of brick in the 1840s.

- **In the 19th century** railroad companies competed to make the grandest, most palatial railroad stations.

- **The Gare d'Orsay** in Paris was an incredibly luxurious station built in 1900 in what is called the *Beaux Arts* (beautiful arts) style. It is now a museum and gallery.

- **When first built** in 1890, Sirkeci in Istanbul—terminal of the Orient Express—glittered like an oriental palace.

- **Mumbai's Victoria**—now Chhatrapati Sivaji—is a palatial gothic station, built in 1888 over a shrine to Mumba Devi, who was the goddess of Mumbai.

- **Grand Central Station** in New York cost a staggering 43 million dollars to build in 1914.

- **Liverpool Street Station** in London was built in 1874 on the site of the 13th century Bedlam hospital for lunatics.

- **London's St. Pancras** is a stunning Gothic building designed by George Gilbert Scott. It was built 1863–72.

- **Chicago's** North Western is a monument to the Jazz Age in the city, dating from 1911.

- **In April 1917** Lenin returned to Russia and announced the start of the Russian revolution at St. Petersburg's famous Finland Railroad station.

▼ *The great hall at Grand Central Station in New York is one of the most spectacular railroad halls in the world.*

Submersibles

- **Submersibles** are small underwater craft. Some are designed for very deep descents for ocean research. Others are designed for exploring wrecks.

- **One early submersible** was a strong metal ball or bathysphere, lowered by cables from a ship.

- **The bathysphere** was built by Americans William Beebe and Otis Barton who went down 2,900ft (900m) in it off Bermuda on June 11, 1931. The possibility of the cable snapping meant the bathysphere was very dangerous.

- **The bathyscaphe** was a diving craft that could be controlled underwater, unlike the bathysphere. Its strong, steel hull could descend 13,123ft (4,000m).

- **The first bathyscaphe**, the FNRS 2, was developed by Swiss scientist August Piccard between 1946 and 1948. An improved version, the FNRS 3, descended 13,123ft (4,000m) off Senegal on February 15, 1954. The FNRS 3 was further improved to make the record-breaking *Trieste*.

- **In the 1960s** the Woods Hole Oceanographic Institute in the U.S. began to develop a smaller, more maneuverable submersible, called *Alvin*. *Alvin* is one of the most famous of all submersibles, making thousands of dives to reveal a huge amount about the ocean depths.

- **ROVs** or Remote Operated Vehicles are small robot submersibles. ROVs are controlled from a ship with video cameras and computer virtual reality systems. ROVs can stay down for days while experts are called in to view results. Using the ROV *Argo-Jason*, Robert Ballard found the wreck of the liner *Titanic* in 1985.

- **Deep Flight** is a revolutionary submersible with wings that can fly underwater like an airplane, turning, diving, banking, and rolling.

- **A new breed** of small submersibles, like the *Sea Star* and *Deep Rover*, cost about the same as a big car and are designed for sports as well as research.

▼ This is one of the first of the huge range of submersibles that began to appear in the 1960s and 70s. They are now much smaller and more maneuverable, but still work in much the same way.

Entry hatch

Searchlights for seeing the dark ocean depths

Claw for grabbing samples

Double hatch containing airlock for divers to go out

Powerful electric motor

Cabin of strong steel to resist intense water pressure

Propeller for pushing the craft through the water

Video camera

Extra strong perspex dome

Batteries

To go back up to the surface, the pilot switches off the electromagnets that hold the ballast of iron balls in place

Float filled with gasoline. Since gasoline is lighter than water, it helps keep the craft afloat

As the craft descends, the gasoline is compressed and gives less buoyancy, speeding the descent

★ STAR FACT ★
On January 23, 1960, the bathyscaphe *Trieste*, controlled by August Piccard's son Jacques, descended a record 35,814ft (10,916m) in the Marianas Trench in the Pacific.

Airports

- **The world's first airport** was built at Croydon near London in 1928. Many early airports, like Berlin's, were social centers attracting thousands of visitors.

- **Before airports,** flying boats would land on water. So airports like New York's La Guardia were set close to water to take flying boats.

- **Over 50 airports** around the world now handle over 10 million passengers a year. 25 of these are in the U.S.

- **Six airports** handle over 30 million passengers, including Chicago's O'Hare and Hong Kong's Chep Lap Kok.

- **The world's largest** airport is King Abdul Aziz in Saudi Arabia. It covers 55,000 acres . The U.S.'s biggest is Dallas. Europe's biggest is Paris's Charles de Gaulle.

- **Hong Kong's** Chep Lap Kok airport, opened in 1998, is one of the world's most modern.

- **Kansai** airport in Japan is built entirely on an artificial island in Osaka Bay so that it can operate 24 hours a day, without disturbing people with noise.

▲ *In the 1970s, Boeing 747 jumbo jets needed runways 2.5mi (4km) long to take-off, but more modern jets now need less space.*

- **In early airports** terminals for each flight were set in a line as at Kansas and Munich. But as flights increased, this layout meant passengers had a long way to walk.

- **Terminals in the 1970s** were set in extending piers like Amsterdam's Schiphol, or satellites like Los Angeles.

- **New airport terminals** like London's Stansted are set apart and linked by electric cars called "people-movers."

Streetcars and cable cars

- **Streetcars** are buses that run on rails laid through city streets. They are called trams in Britain.

- **Early streetcars** in the 1830s were pulled by horses. By the 1870s, horse-drawn streetcars were widely used.

- **In 1834** Thomas Davenport, a blacksmith from Vermont, built a battery-powered electric streetcar.

- **In 1860** an American called George Train set up battery-powered electric streetcar systems in London.

- **In 1873** Andrew Hallidie introduced cable cars in San Francisco. The cars were hauled by a cable running in a slot in the street. A powerhouse pulled the cable at around 8.5mph (14km/h). Similar systems were built in many cities but were soon replaced by electric streetcars.

- **In 1888** Frank Sprague demonstrated a streetcar run from electric overhead cables in Richmond.

- **In most U.S. streetcars,** electric current was picked up via a long pole with a small wheel called a shoe that slid along the cable. The pick-up was called a trolley.

Many European streetcars, however, picked up current via a collapsible frame called a pantograph.

- **In the early 1900s,** electric streetcar systems were set up in most world cities.

  - **In the 1930s** most cities, except in eastern Europe and Russia, replaced streetcars with buses.

  - **In the 1990s** some cities, like Manchester in England, built new streetcar systems, as they are fume-free.

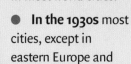

◄ *The original Hallidie cable car system dating from 1873 still runs in San Francisco.*

The Wright brothers

- **The Wright brothers,** Orville and Wilbur, built the world's first successful plane, the *Flyer.*

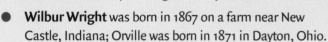

- **On December 17, 1903** the Wright brothers made the first powered, long, and controlled airplane flight at Kitty Hawk.

- **Wilbur Wright** was born in 1867 on a farm near New Castle, Indiana; Orville was born in 1871 in Dayton, Ohio.

- **The Wright brothers** began as bicyclemakers but became keen on flying after hearing about the death of pioneer glider Otto Lilienthal in 1896.

- **From 1899 to 1903** they worked at Kitty Hawk methodically improving their design and flying skill.

- ◀ One of the five who witnessed the flight took this picture. But the Wrights' success was little known for five years.

- **Many early planes** lacked control. The key to the Wrights' success was stopping the plane from rolling, using wires to "warp" (twist) the wings to lift one side or the other.

- **The *Flyer*'s** wing warp meant it could not only fly level but make balanced, banked turns (like a bicycle cornering).

- **For the first flight** Orville was at the controls.

- **The historic first flight** lasted 12 seconds, in which the *Flyer* traveled 120ft (37m) and landed safely.

- **On October 5, 1905** the Wrights flew 24mi (39km/h) in 38 mins.

Bicycles

▲ Bicycles are the cheapest, most reliable form of transportation ever. In the 1920s many tradesmen adapted them for use.

- **The first bicycle** was the "draisienne" of 1818 of Baron de Drais. The rider scooted his feet on the ground to move.

- **In 1839** Scots blacksmith Kirkpatrick Macmillan invented the first bicycle with pedals and brakes.

- **On Macmillan's "velocipede"** pedals were linked by rods to cranks on the back wheel. These turned the wheel slowly.

- **In 1861** French father and son Pierre and Ernest Michaux stuck the pedals directly on the front wheel to make the first successful bicycle, nicknamed "boneshaker."

- **In 1870** James Starley improved the boneshaker with the Ordinary. A huge front wheel gave high speed with little pedaling.

- **In 1874** H. J. Lawson made the first chain-driven bicycle. This was called a "safety bicycle" because it was safer than the tall Ordinary.

- **In 1885** Starley's nephew John made the Rover Safety bicycle. Air-filled tires were added in 1890, and the modern bicycle was born.

- **By 1895** four million Americans were riding bicycles.

- **Today** 50 million people in the U.S. cycle regularly.

- **More people** in China cycle today than the rest of the world put together.

Great voyages

▶ In 1580, Sir Francis Drake became the first Englishman to sail round the world. En route, he visited what is now California.

● **In 330BC** the Greek sailor Pytheas sailed out into the Atlantic through the Straits of Gibraltar and found his way to "Thule" (Britain).

● **Around AD1000** the Viking Leif Ericsson was the first European to cross the Atlantic to North America.

● **In 1405** Chinese admiral Cheng Ho began a series of seven epic voyages around the Indian Ocean in a huge fleet of junks.

● **In 1492** Genoese Christopher Columbus crossed the Atlantic from Cadiz in Spain and discovered the New World. His ship was the *Santa Maria*.

> ★ STAR FACT ★
> In 1522, Ferdinand Magellan's ship *Victoria* made the first round-the-world voyage.

● **From 1499–1504** Italian Amerigo Vespucci sailed the Atlantic and realized South America was a continent. America is named after him.

● **In 1492** Italian John Cabot crossed the North Atlantic from Bristol in England and found Canada.

● **In 1498** Portuguese Vasco da Gama was the first European to reach India by sea, sailing all around Africa.

● **In 1642** Dutchman Abel Tasman sailed to what is now Australia and New Zealand. The island of Tasmania is named after him.

● **From 1768–79** James Cook explored the South Pacific in his ship the *Endeavour* and landed at Botany Bay.

▶ Between 1492 and 1504, Colombus explored the West Indies and the coasts of Central and South America.

Ancient palaces

● **The word palace** comes from the Palatine Hill in Rome, where the emperors of Rome had their palaces.

● **The earliest known** palaces are those built in Thebes in Ancient Egypt by King Thutmose III in the 15th century BC.

● **Egyptian palaces** had a rectangular wall enclosing a maze of small rooms and a courtyard—a pattern later followed by many Asian palaces.

● **The Babylonians** and Persians introduced grand halls in their palaces at Susa and elsewhere.

● **Minoan palaces** on Crete introduced extra stories.

● **Roman palaces** were the grandest of the ancient world.

● **The Sacred Palace** of Byzantium (now Istanbul) was biggest of all, covering 3,595,000 sq ft (334,000 sq m).

● **Palaces** in China and Japan, like Beijing's Forbidden City, often had a high wall surrounding small houses for the ruler and his officials.

● **Ancient palaces in the Americas** like the Mayan palace at Uxmal dating from AD900, are usually simpler.

● **Potala palace** stands high above Lhasa in Tibet. Potala means "high heavenly realm." The original, built by King Srong-brtsan-sgam-po in the 7th century was destroyed by the Chinese c.1600. The Dalai Lama rebuilt it in 1645.

◀ The 12th-century Khmer emperors of Cambodia built magnificent palaces in their capital of Angkor, now overgrown by jungle. But most magnificent of all was the temple, Angkor Wat.

Docks and ports

- **Some ports** like Hong Kong and Rio, are based on natural harbors; others are constructed artificially.

- **The Phoenicians** built artificial harbors at Tyre and Sidon in the Lebanon in the 13th century.

- **The Romans** invented waterproof concrete to build the quays and breakwaters at their port of Ostia.

- **Roman and other ancient ports** had animal and human powered cranes. Saxon London and Viking Dublin had well-built wooden wharves.

- **Traditionally,** big boats would anchor in midstream and barges called lighters would take the cargo ashore.

- **In the 18th century** the first enclosed deep water docks were built at London and Liverpool. Here big ships could moor and unload directly onto the wharves.

> ★ STAR FACT ★
> The world's busiest ports are Rotterdam, Singapore, and Hong Kong.

- **In the 20th century,** ports specializing in particular cargoes, such as oil terminals, grew.

- **Since the 1950s** there has been a huge growth in container ports. Containers are big, standardized metal crates that can be loaded on and off quickly.

- **The world's main container ports** are Hong Kong, Singapore, Rotterdam, Hamburg, and New York.

▲ The port of Balstad in Norway is a perfect natural harbor.

Modern architecture

▶ The old and new in Hong Kong: the ultra modern Hong Kong-Shanghai bank dwarfs a 19th-century classical building.

- **In the 1920s** many architects rejected old styles to experiment with simple shapes in materials like glass, steel, and concrete.

- **The International Style** was pioneered by Swiss architect Le Corbusier who built houses in smooth geometric shapes like boxes.

- **The Bauhaus** school in Germany believed buildings should look like the job they were meant to do.

- **Walter Gropius** and Mies van de Rohe brought Bauhaus ideas to the U.S. and developed sleek, glass-walled, steel-framed skyscrapers like New York's Seagram Building.

- **American Frank Lloyd Wright** (1869-1959) was famous both for his low, prairie-style bungalows "growing" from their site and his airy and elegant geometric buildings.

- **In the 1950s** architects like Kenzo Tange of Japan reacted against the "blandness" of the International Style, introducing a rough concrete look called Brutalism.

- **In the 1960s** many critics reacted against the damage done by modern architecture to historic cities.

- **Post-modernists** were united in rejecting modern architecture, often reviving historical styles. American Robert Venturi added traditional decoration.

- **Richard Rogers's** and Renzo Piano's Pompidou Centre in Paris (1977) was a humorous joke on the Bauhaus idea, exposing the "bones" of the building.

- **With shiny metal** and varied shapes, the Guggenheim gallery in Bilbao in Spain is a new masterpiece.

Pyramids

- **Pyramids** are huge ancient monuments with a square base and triangular sides coming together in a point at the top. Remarkably, they are found not only in Egypt, but also in Greece, Cyprus, Italy, India, Thailand, Mexico, South America, and various Pacific islands.

- **The earliest tombs** of the pharaohs were mud chambers called mastabas. But c.2686BC, the architect Imhotep had a pyramid-shaped tomb built for Zoser at Saqqara. This rose in steps and so is called the Step Pyramid.

- **In 2600BC** the Egyptians filled in the steps on a pyramid with stones to make the first smooth pyramid at Medum.

- **The ruins of 80 pyramids** stand near the Nile in Egypt, built over 1,000 years. Each has an elaborate system of hidden passageways and chambers to stop robbers getting at the tomb of the pharaoh inside.

- **The largest pyramid** is the Great Pyramid at Giza, built for the Pharaoh Khufu c.2551–2472BC. This was once 482ft (147m) high, but is now 460ft (140m), since some upper stones have been lost.

▶ *The strange half lion, half pharaoh statue called the Sphinx stands near the pyramid of pharaoh Khafre at Giza.*

- **Later the Egyptians** abandoned pyramids and cut tombs into rock, as in the Valley of Kings at Thebes. The tomb of Tutankhamun was one of these.

- **The Moche Indians** of Peru built large brick pyramids, including the Pyramid of the Sun near Trujillo.

- **Another Pyramid of the Sun** is on the site of the ancient Aztec capital of Teotihuacan, 30mi (50km) from Mexico City. Built around 2,000 years ago, it is exactly the same size, 2,475 sq ft (230 sq m), as the Great Pyramid at Giza.

- **The American pyramids** were not tombs like those in Egypt, but temples, so they have no hidden chambers inside. They are built not from blocks of cut stone but from millions of basketloads of volcanic ash and gravel.

> ★ STAR FACT ★
> The Great Pyramid at Giza was made of
> 2.3 million 2.5-ton blocks of limestone.

▶ *No one knows just how the Egyptians managed to build such huge structures as the pyramids. It is thought that over 100,000 people worked on each big pyramid. Each block was probably cut from the quarry, dragged on rollers to the River Nile, and carried by barge to the building site. The stones were then dragged into place up earth ramps.*

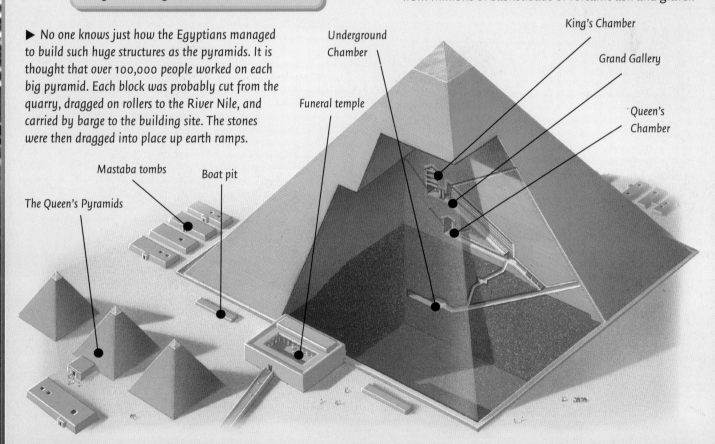

Underground Chamber

King's Chamber

Grand Gallery

Funeral temple

Queen's Chamber

Mastaba tombs

Boat pit

The Queen's Pyramids

Moving on snow

▲ *Cutters are still used in the north-eastern U.S. as a charming way of getting around in the winter snows.*

- **Vehicles** designed to move on snow are supported on flat boards called runners, skids, or skis. These slide over snow and spread the vehicle's weight over a larger area.

- **Sleds or sleighs** drawn by horses or dogs may have been the first vehicles ever used by humans.

- **Cutters** are light, graceful horse-drawn sleighs first introduced in the U.S. about 1800.

- **Troikas** are Russian sleighs (or carriages) drawn by three horses. The middle horse is supposed to trot while the outer horses gallop in particular ways.

- **Native Americans** had toboggans made of poles tied with leather thongs.

- **Snowmobiles** are vehicles with two skis at the front and a motor-driven track roll at the back. Racing snowmobiles can reach over 100mph (160km/h).

- **Snowmobiles** are steered by handlebars that control the skis and by the shifting of the driver's weight.

- **The first propeller-driven** snowmobile was built in the 1920s. Tracked snowmobiles were developed in 1959 by Canadian Joseph Bombardier.

- **In the 1960s,** carved wooden skis dating back 8,000 years were found in a bog at Vis near the Urals in Russia.

- **Early skates** were mostly small bone skis tied to the feet.

Rescue boats

- **Several designs** for "unsinkable" lifeboats were tried in 18th-century France and England.

- **After many drowned** when the ship *Adventure* went down in 1789, a contest for a lifeboat was set up.

- **The contest winner** was Newcastle boatbuilder Henry Greathead. His boat the *Original* would right itself when capsized and still float even when nearly filled with water.

- **The first land-based** powered lifeboat was steam-powered, launched in 1890.

- **Around 1907** diesel-power lifeboats were introduced. Without the need for oars,

▶ *This is a typical inflatable inshore rescue boat. Boats like these are bonded together by heat and glue, and are incredibly tough.*

most of the boat could be covered in and so made even more unsinkable.

- **Modern land-based lifeboats** are either steel-hulled or made of a double skin of timber.

- **The hull** usually contains a large number of sealed air containers so it is almost impossible for the boat to sink.

- **Some lifeboats** are afloat all the time. Others are kept ashore in a lifeboat house ready for emergencies.

- **Lifeboats** kept ashore are launched down a slipway into the ocean or wheeled into the ocean on a cradle until they float.

- **As leisure sailing** and swimming has increased, so there has been an increase in the number of inshore rescue boats. These are small rubber or fiberglass boats, kept afloat by an inflatable tube of toughened rubber.

Famous trains

- **Pullman coaches** became a byword for luxury in the United States in the 1860s.

- **After a trip to the U.S.,** young Belgian George Nagelmackers set up the Wagon-Lits company to do in Europe as Pullman had in the U.S.

- **The most famous** Wagon-Lits was the luxurious *Orient Express* from Paris to Istanbul, which started in 1883.

- **Among the many famous** travelers on the *Orient Express* were the female spy Mata Hari, the fictional spy James Bond, and 40s film star Marlene Dietrich.

- **Another famous** Wagon-Lits train is the *Trans-Siberian Express,* set up in 1898.

- **The** *Trans-Siberian* takes eight days to go right across Russia and Siberia from Moscow to Vladivostok.

▲ *The Orient Express gained the glamour of intrigue after Agatha Christie wrote "Murder on the Orient Express."*

> ★ **STAR FACT** ★
> At 5,864mi (9,438km), the *Trans-Siberian Express* is the world's longest train journey.

- **The** *Flying Scotsman* was famed for its fast, nonstop runs from London to Edinburgh in the 1920s.

- **The** *Golden Arrow* ran from London to Paris.

- **The** *Indian Pacific* in Australia runs on the world's longest track, 297mi (478km) across the Nullarbor Plain.

Sailing and tacking

- **Sailing ships** can sail into the wind because the wind does not so much push the sail as suck it.

- **The sail** is always angled so that the wind blows across it, allowing it to act like the wing of an aircraft.

- **As the wind blows** over the curve of the sail, it speeds up and its pressure drops in front of the sail. The extra pressure of the other side drives the boat forward.

- **The sail** works as long as the wind is blowing straight across it, so to go in a particular direction, the sailor simply changes the angle of the sail.

- **The boat's keel,** or centerboard, stops it from slipping sideways.

▲ *With their sails in line with the hull, these yachts are sailing close to the wind.*

- **The boat can sail** with the wind behind it, to the side of it, or even slightly ahead of it.

- **To sail directly** into the wind, a boat has to "tack." This means zigzagging back and forth across the path of the wind, so wind is always blowing across the sails.

- **At the end** of each tack, the sail "comes about" (changes course). The tiller (steering arm) is turned to point the boat on the new course and the sail is allowed to "gybe" (swing over to the other side).

- **Sailing close to the wind** is sailing nearly into the wind.

- **Running with the wind** is sailing with a fast wind behind.

Airships

Rigid envelope shell

Envelope filled with helium

▼ This is a cutaway of one of the new breed of small airships made from lightweight materials and filled with safe, non flammable helium gas.

Airbags or "ballonets" inside the helium-filled envelope. As the airship climbs, air pressure drops and the helium expands, pushing air out of the ballonets. As the airship drops again, the helium contracts and air is let into the ballonets again

Valve to let air in and out of the ballonets

Elevator flaps to help climbing or diving

Gondola where pilot sits

Landing wheel

Propeller powered by a car engine

Rudder to steer the airship to the left or right

- **By the mid-1800s** ballooning was a popular activity, but balloons have to float where the wind takes them. So in 1852, French engineer Henri Giffard made a cigar-shaped balloon filled with the very light gas hydrogen. He powered it with a steam-driven propeller and added a rudder to make it more "dirigible" or steerable.

- **In 1884** two French inventors, Charles Renard and Arthur Krebs, built the first really dirigible balloon, *La France.* This was powered by an electric motor.

- **In 1897** Austrian David Schwartz gave a powered, cigar-shaped balloon a rigid frame to create the first airship.

- **In 1900** Count Ferdinand von Zeppelin built the first of his huge airships, the 420ft (128m) long LZ-1.

- **In 1909** Zeppelin helped set up the wold's first airline, DELAG, flying 485ft (148m) long airships, carrying 10,000 passengers in their first four years.

- **In World War I,** Germany used Zeppelin airships to make the first aerial bombing raids.

- **By the 1920s** vast airships were carrying people back and forth across the Atlantic in the style of a luxury ocean liner. The *Graf Zeppelin* flew at 80mph (130km/h). In its gondola, 60 or more passengers sat in comfortable lounges and cocktail bars, listening to bands playing.

- **On May 6, 1937** disaster struck the 800ft (245m) long airship *Hindenburg* as it docked at Lakehurst, New Jersey. The hydrogen in its balloon caught fire and exploded, killing 35 people. The day of the airship was over.

- **In recent years** there has been a revival of airships for advertising, filled with safer helium gas. Most are non rigid, but Airship Industries Skyship is semi rigid and made from modern, light material, such as carbon fiber.

> ★ STAR FACT ★
> Fighter planes could take off from and land
> on the 1930s airship *Akron* in mid-air.

Underground railroads

- **Underground railroads** are also called subways, metros, or even just tubes.
- **There are three kinds:** open-cut, cut-and-cover, and tube.
- **Open-cut subways** are built by digging rectangular ditches in streets, like much of New York's subway.
- **Cut-and-cover subways** are when an open-cut subway is covered again with a road or sidewalk.
- **Tubes** are deep, round tunnels created by boring through the ground, like most of London's lines.
- **The world's first underground** was the cut-and-cover Metropolitan Line in London, opened on January 10, 1863, using steam engines.
- **In 1890** the world's first electric tube trains ran on London's first deep tube, the City and South London.
- **After 1900** American Charles Yerkes, builder of the Chicago Loop railway, gave London the world's most extensive network with 140mi (225km) of deep tubes.

▲ London was the first city in the world to have an underground system. Much of it is now in deep tube tunnels.

- **Moscow's Metro** grand stations were built in the 1930s with marble, stained glass, statues, and chandeliers.
- **New York City** has the world's largest subway network. The first line opened on October 27, 1904.

The Eiffel Tower

- **The Eiffel Tower** in Paris was 1,025ft (312.2m) high when it was first built. An antenna brings it up to 1,045ft (318.7m). There are 1,665 steps up to the top.
- **On a clear day** you can see 50mi (80km) in all directions from the top. It is often sunny at the top when the weather in the Paris streets is cloudy.
- **It was made** from 18,038 pieces of iron, held together by 2,500,000 rivets.
- **It was built in 1889** for the exhibition celebrating the 100th anniversary of the French Revolution.
- **Gustave Eiffel** (1832–1923) was the most successful engineer of the day, building not only the Eiffel Tower but New York's Statue of Liberty too.

▲ Paris's Eiffel Tower is one of the world's most famous landmarks.

- **The Eiffel Tower** was designed by Maurice Koechlin and Emile Nougier who calculated the effects of wind and gravity with amazing precision.
- **The Tower** was intended to show what could be done with cast iron.
- **During building work** Parisian artists, such as the composer Gounod and poet Maupassant, protested against its ugliness. But when completed it was an instant success.
- **The cost of building** the Eiffel Tower was over $1 million. However, the fees from the visitors in the first year alone covered the construction costs.
- **When Paris was occupied** by the Nazis during the war, the elevators "mysteriously" stopped working. They restarted the day Paris was liberated.

Missiles

★ STAR FACT ★
American Tomahawk cruise missiles could be aimed through goalposts at both ends of a football field 300mi (500km) away.

Explosive warhead

Solid rocket fuel

▶ *90 percent of the weight of a ballistic missile is the rocket propellant needed to reach its distant target.*

- **In AD1232** the Chinese defended the city of K'ai-feng against the Mongols with gunpowder rockets.

- **In the early 1800s** British army officer William Congreve developed metal rockets carrying explosives.

- **In World War II** the Germans developed the first guided missiles—missiles steered to their target in flight.

- **The most frightening** German guided missiles were the V-1 flying bombs or "doodlebugs" and the V2 supersonic rockets. The V-2s flew at 3,295mph (5,300km/h).

- **Ballistic missiles** arch through the air like a thrown ball. Rockets propel them on the upward trajectory (path). They then coast down on their target. Cruise missiles are propelled by jet on a low flat path all the way.

- **In the 1950s** the U.S. and Soviet Union competed to develop long-range ICBMs (Intercontinental Ballistic Missiles) armed with nuclear warheads.

- **In the 1960s** antiballistic missiles were developed to shoot down missiles.

- **Some ICBMs** have a range of over 3,000mi (5,000km). Short range missiles (SRBMs) like Pershings reach up to 300mi (500km).

- **SAMS** (surface-to-air missiles) like Redeye are fired from the ground at aircraft. AAMs (air-to-air missiles) like Sidewinders are fired from planes against other planes.

Ancient America

- **The largest buildings** in Ancient America were Mayan pyramids, like the Tomb of Pakal in South Mexico.

- **Teotihuacan** in Mexico is one of the best preserved ancient cities in the world, with its magnificent pyramids, palaces, temples, courts, and homes.

- **At its height** around 2,000 years ago, Teotihuacan was the world's biggest city with 100,000 people.

- **Hopewell Indians** of Newark, Ohio built earthwork tombs in AD250 that rivaled Egypt's pyramids in size.

★ STAR FACT ★
The Incas built 15,500mi (25,000km) of stone-paved roads between 1450 and 1532.

- **Aztecs** built the Great Temple pyramid in their ancient capital of Tenochtitlan (now Mexico City) from 1325–1500. Human sacrifices were made at the top.

- **The Mesa Verde** is a famous "pueblo" (stone village) of the Anasazi in New Mexico, abandoned around AD1100.

- **In the Chaco Canyon** the Anasazi built 400mi (650km) of mysterious roads to nowhere.

- **Nazca Lines** are huge outlines of birds, monkeys, and other things up to 325ft (100m) across, drawn by Nazca people of southern Peru. They date from c.100BC to AD700.

- **The Nazca Lines** are only clearly seen from the air. They may have been part of a giant astronomical calendar.

◀ *The 1,500-year-old pyramids of the Maya were once overgrown by jungle, but most have now been revealed.*

Palaces

- **The palaces** of Europe owe much to the vast palaces of the caliphs of the Near East, built in 7th and 8th centuries, with their cool courtyards and rich decoration.

- **The Topkapi Palace** in Istanbul was the sumptuous home of the Ottoman sultans for over 400 years until it was made into a museum in 1924, after the sultans' fall.

- **Venice's Doge's Palace** (mainly 1400s) shows oriental touches bought from the east by Venetian merchants.

- **The elegant Pitti Palace** in Florence was designed by the brilliant architect Brunelleschi for the merchant Luca Pitti in 1440. It was taken over by the Medici family in 1550.

- **Hampton Court Palace** , south of London, was begun in 1514 by King Henry VIII's favorite Cardinal Wolsey—but when Wolsey fell from favor, the King took it over.

- **The Escorial** in Madrid is a massive granite palace built by Philip II. It was begun in 1563 and completed in 1584.

- **Many 18th-century princes** built their own lavish palaces like those at Dresden in Germany, Vienna's

▲ London's Buckingham Palace is the home of the Queen of Britain.

Schönbrunn, and St. Petersburg's Winter Palace.

- **Buckingham House**, London, built in 1705 for the Duke of Buckingham, was remodeled as a palace in 1825.

- **Inspired by English gardens,** Peter the Great made Russia's oldest garden, the Summer Garden in St. Petersburg in 1710, in which he built the Summer Palace.

- **Catherine the Great** had the St. Petersburg's Winter Palace built by architect Bartolomeo Rastrelli in 1762.

First steamships

- **In 1783** French nobleman Marquis Claude de Jouffroy d'Abbans built a huge steam boat that churned up the Saone River near Lyon in France for 15 minutes before the pounding engines shook it to pieces.

- **In 1787** American John Fitch made the first successful steamship with an engine driving a series of paddles.

- **In 1790** Fitch started the world's first steam service on the Delaware River.

- **In 1802** Scot William Symington built a tug, the *Charlotte Dundas*, able to tow two 70-ton barges.

- **In 1807** American Robert Fulton made the first steam passenger boats running 150mi (240km) up the Hudson River.

- **In 1819** the New York-built ship *Savannah* made the first steam-assisted crossing of the Atlantic.

- **In 1833** Canadian ship *Royal William* made the first mainly steam-powered Atlantic crossing in two days.

- **In 1843** British engineer Isembard Kingdom Brunel launched the first all-iron hull steamship, the *Great Britain*.

- **In 1858** Brunel launched *Great Eastern*, the biggest ship of the 19th century, 692ft (211m) long, and weighing 30,000 tons.

- **Early steamships** had paddles, but in 1835 Swede John Ericsson invented a screw propeller.

◄ Steam-driven warships like this, HMS Theseus, were built in the 1800s.

Taking off

- **An aircraft's wings** or "foils" are lifted by the air flowing around them as they slice through the air.

- **Because the top** of the wing is curved, air pushed over the wing speeds up and stretches out. The stretching of the air reduces its pressure.

- **Underneath the wing** air slows down and bunches up, so air pressure here rises.

- **The wing gains "lift"** as the wing is sucked from above and pushed from below.

★ STAR FACT ★
Slots on the wing's leading edge smooth airflow to increase the safe angle of attack.

- **The amount of lift** depends on the angle of the wing—called the angle of attack—and its shape, and also how fast it is moving through the air.

- **Aircraft** get extra lift for climbing by increasing their speed through the air and by dropping the tail so that the main wings cut through the air at a steeper angle.

- **If the angle of attack** becomes too steep, the air flow breaks up and the wing loses lift. This is called a stall.

- **Planes** take off when air is moving fast enough over the wing to provide enough lift.

- **Airliners** have "high-lift" slots and flaps on the wings to give extra lift for slow takeoff and landing speeds.

◀ *The high-lift flaps are down to give extra lift on a climb.*

The Taj Mahal

- **The Taj Mahal** (said *tarj m'hal*) in Agra in India is perhaps the most beautiful tomb in the world.

- **Mughal Indian** ruler Shah Jehan ordered it to be built in honor of his favorite wife Mumtaz Mahal, who died giving birth to their 14th child.

- **Mumtaz** died in 1629, and the Taj was built over 22 years from 1632 to 1653.

- **The Taj** is set at the north end of a formal Persian garden with water courses and rows of cypress trees.

- **It is made of white** marble and sits on a platform of sandstone.

- **Inside,** behind an octagonal screen, lie the jewel-inlaid cenotaphs (tombs) of Mumtaz and

Shah Jehan. The Shah was placed there when he died. His tomb is the only asymmetrical feature in the Taj.

- **20,000 workers** worked in marble and sandstone, silver, gold, carnelian, jasper, moonstone, jade, lapis lazuli, and coral to enhance the Taj's beauty.

- **At each corner** of the platform is a slender minaret 133ft (40.5m) tall.

- **In the center** is a dome 70ft (21.3m) across and 120ft (36.6m) high.

- **The main architect** was Iranian Isa Khan, but the decorations were said to be by Austin of Bordeaux and Veroneo of Venice.

◀ *So perfect are the Taj's proportions that it was said to have been designed by giants and finished by jewelers.*

Jet engines

Front fan to create "cold" bypass stream

The engine casing is made of carbon fiber and plastic honeycomb for lightness. Inside is an outer bypass duct for the "cold-stream" of air from the front fan. An inner duct takes the "hot stream" through the compressor, combustion chamber, and turbine to create the exhaust

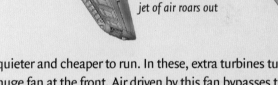

▶ All but the very fastest warplanes are powered by turbofan jet engines, like this Russian MiG. Turbofans first came into widespread use in the 1970s and are now by far the most common kind of jet engine.

Air intake

Exhaust where a hot jet of air roars out

- **A kind of jet engine** was built by the Ancient Greek Hero of Alexander in the first century AD. It was a ball driven around by jets of steam escaping from two nozzles.

- **The first jet engines** were built at the same time in the 1930s by Pabst von Ohain in Germany and Frank Whittle in Britain—though neither knew of the other's work.

> ★ STAR FACT ★
> In a typical turbojet, exhaust gases roar from the engine at over 1,000mph (1,600km/h).

- **Ohain's engine** was put in the Heinkel HE-178 which first flew on August 27, 1939; Whittle's was put in the Gloster E28 of 1941. The first American experimental jet was the Bell XP-59 Aircomet of 1942.

- **Jets** work by pushing a jet of air out the back. This hits the air so fast that the reaction thrusts the plane forward like a deflating balloon.

- **Jet engines** are also called gas turbines because they burn fuel gas to spin the blades of a turbine non-stop.

- **Turbojets** are the original form of jet engine. Air is scooped in at the front and squeezed by spinning "compressor" blades. Fuel sprayed into the squeezed air in the middle of the engine burns, making the mixture expand dramatically. The expanding air not only pushes round turbines which drive the compressor, but also sends out a high-speed jet of hot air to propel the plane. This high-speed jet is noisy but good for ultra-fast warplanes and the supersonic Concorde.

- **Turboprops** are turbojets that use most of their power to turn a propeller rather than force out a hot air jet.

- **Turbofans** are used by most airliners because they are

quieter and cheaper to run. In these, extra turbines turn a huge fan at the front. Air driven by this fan bypasses the engine core and gives a huge extra boost at low speeds.

- **Ramjets** or "flying stovepipes" are the simplest type of jet engine, used only on missiles. They dispense with both compressor and turbine blades and simply rely on the speed of the jet through the air to ram air in through the intake into the engine.

▶ Like nearly all warplanes today, "stealth" aircraft are jet-propelled. But the afterburner stream of hot gases from the jets provides a "signature" that can show up all too clearly on some detection equipment. So stealth aircraft are designed to "supercruise," that is, fly at supersonic speeds without much afterburn.

Yachts and catamarans

▲ *Catamarans with twin hulls and outriggers (extra floats) are all developed from traditional Polynesian outriggers.*

- **The word yacht** comes from the 17th-century Dutch word *jacht*, which meant "ship for chasing."

- **English yachting** began in 1662 when King Charles II raced his brother James on the Thames for a £100 bet in a small pleasure boat given to him by the Dutch.

- **In 1898** Joshua Slocum sailed single-handed round

the world in the 37ft (11.3m) *Spray*, proving the seaworthiness of small craft.

- **From the 1920s** the same aerodynamic principles applied to hulls were used for sails and rigging.

- **Most racing yachts** are now built from aluminum and light, strong composites such as carbon fiber.

- **In the 1960s** twin-hulled catamarans became popular since they pierce waves well yet are wide and stable.

- **In 1983** Australian Ben Lexcen became the first non-American to win the famous America's Cup race.

- **The key to Lexcen's** success was revolutionary winglets on the keel to improve stability.

- **Sails on some yachts** are now computer-controled to keep them at exactly the right angle.

> **! NEWS FLASH !**
> America's Cup yachts have winglets on their rudder and keels for extra stability.

Powerboats

- **Powerboating** began in 1863 when Frenchman Jean Lenoir installed a gasoline engine in a small boat.

- **The first major race** was in 1903 across the English Channel. The Gold Cup, organized by the American Power Boat Association, started on the Hudson in 1904.

- **About 1910** motormakers like Evinrude introduced detachable "outboard" motors that clamp to the stern. Inboard motors have the engine built into the hull.

- **In the 1920s** racing boats adopted "planing hulls" for skimming across the water at high speeds, rather than traditional, deep v-shaped "displacement" hulls.

▼ *Powerboat racing has become as competitive as motor racing. Formula One boats reach speeds of over 125mph (200km/h).*

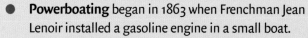

After World War II, hulls were made more and more not from wood, but from metals and fiberglass.

- **Most powerboats** are driven by a high-speed jet of water, as opposed to by a propeller screw.

- **In 1994** American Tom Gentry set the offshore Class 1 record of 157.4mph (253.35km/h) in Skater powerboats.

- **In 1996** Gentry's *Gentry Eagle* crossed the Atlantic in 2 days 14 hours 7 mins. In 1997, the skipper *Destriero* made it in 2 days 6 hours 34 mins.

- **The official water speed** record is 317.58mph (511.11km/h) by Kenneth Warby in his hydroplane *Spirit of Australia* on Blowering Lake, New South Wales on October 8, 1978.

- **Jet skis** are like motorboats that skim across the water on a ski. They were developed by the American Clayton Jacobsen back in the 1960s.

- **The jet ski** speed record is 43mph (69km/h) by French D. Condemine in 1994 on a Yahama.

Biplanes

- **Most early planes** were biplanes (doublewingers) or even triplanes (triplewingers).

- **Monoplanes** (singlewingers) like Blériot's (see Record-breaking flights) won many early races, because they did not drag on the air like multiwings.

- **Accidents** by overstressed competition monoplanes made it look as if they were dangerous. Single wings were weak, it seemed, because they had to be very long to give a similar lifting area to multiwings.

- **In 1912** the French and British banned monoplanes, so all World War I fighter planes were multiwingers.

- **Biplane wings** were strong because struts and wires linked the small, light wings to combine their strength.

- **Famous World War I** fighters included the British Sopwith Camel and Bristol Fighter.

◀ *The biplanes of World War I were slow but highly maneuverable. Pilots were able to show tremendous flying skill in the first aerial "dog fights" between planes.*

- **The Fokker triplane** flown by German air ace Baron von Richtofen (the Red Baron) was said to be "fearsome to look at and climbs like an elevator."

- **With their network** of struts and wires, biplanes were affectionately known as "string bags."

- **In the years** after World War I, huge biplane airliners were built, including the Handley Page Heracles.

- **By the late 1920s** planes could be built strongly all in metal. So, to cut drag and boost speed, designers went back to monoplanes, such as the Supermarine S6B. Soon biplanes seemed old-fashioned.

The Palace of Versailles

▲ *Versailles is perhaps the most expensive palace ever built.*

- **Versailles,** in France, is a magnificent palace built for Louis XIV. Work began in 1661 and carried on for a century.

- **When complete** Versailles was 1,640ft (500m) long, had over 1,300 rooms, and could accommodate 5,000 people.

- **The first architect** was Louis le Vau but Jules Hardouin-Mansart took over in 1676, adding the second story.

- **The interior** was conceived by Charles le Brun. His Hall of Mirrors is a long hall lined with mirrors. A masterly painted ceiling shows Louis XIV's achievements.

- **Throughout Versailles** high ceilings and great doors are emblazoned in gold with the mark of the sun god, Apollo, and of King Louis, known as the Sun King.

- **The huge gardens** of tree-lined terraces and ponds were landscaped by Andre le Notre with 1,400 fountains, 400 new pieces of sculpture, and four million tulips.

- **The fountains** appear "magically" still to show the power of the king over nature.

- **The palace** had a famous state-of-the-art theater designed by Jacques-Ange Gabriel in 1769.

- **During the French Revolution** on October 6, 1789, mobs invaded the palace and wrecked its interiors. Restoration began in 1837 and has continued ever since.

- **The avenues of Washington D.C.** were laid out in imitation of Versailles by a French architect.

Trains of the future

▲ *Many cities now have short monorails, but they seem unlikely to get much bigger because of the disruption building would cause.*

- **Monorails** are single beam tracks raised over city streets.

- **The first monorail** was built in Wuppertal, Germany as long ago as 1901. Monorails have been seen as trains of the future ever since.

- **Monorails** of the future may be air-cushion trains or maglev, as at Birmingham airport in England.

- **A maglev** is proposed in Japan to take passengers the 320mi (515km) from Tokyo to Osaka in under 60 minutes. Germany's version is called *Transrapid*.

- **PRT** or Personalized Rapid Transport is a system of small vehicles that run on elevated tracks at high speed.

- **185mph (300km/h)** High Speed Train (HST) systems like the French *TGV* are being built in many places. A line from Moscow to St. Petersburg was opened in 2000.

- **In 2004** the 200mph (320km/h) Tampa to Miami Florida *Overland Express* opens. The same year a 3,000mi (4,500km), 185mph (300km/h) line may also open from Melbourne to Darwin, Australia.

- **Most HSTs** run on special straight tracks. Tilting trains lean into bends to give high speeds on winding old tracks.

- **Tilting trains** include the 185mph (300km/h) Italian Fiat *Pendolini* and the Swedish *X2000*.

- **The 150mph (240km/h)** tilting train *The American Flyer*—Washington to Baltimore—is the U.S.'s fastest train.

Rockets

> **· STAR FACT ·**
> The *Saturn V* rocket that launched the Apollo mission to the Moon is the most powerful rocket ever built.

- **Rockets** work by burning fuel. As fuel burns and swells out behind, the swelling pushes the rocket forward.

- **Solid-fuel rockets** are the oldest of all engines, used by the Chinese a thousand years ago.

- **Solid-fuel engines** are basically rods of solid, rubbery

◄ *Only powerful rockets can give the thrust to overcome gravity and launch spacecraft into space. They fall away in stages once the spacecraft is traveling fast enough.*

fuel with a tube down the middle.

- **Solid fuel** rockets are usually only used for model rockets and small booster rockets. But the Space Shuttle has two solid rocket boosters (SRBs) as well as three main liquid fuel engines.

- **Most powerful launch rockets** use liquid fuel. The Shuttle uses hydrogen. Other fuels include kerosene.

- **Liquid fuel** only burns with oxygen, so rockets must also carry an oxidizer (a substance that gives oxygen) such as liquid oxygen (LOX) or nitrogen tetroxide.

- **Future rocket drives** include nuclear thermal engines that would use a nuclear reactor to heat the gas blasted out.

- **NASA's Deep Space-1** project is based on xenon ion engines which thrust, not hot gases out the back, but electrically charged particles called ions.

- **Solar thermal engines** of the future would collect the Sun's rays with a large mirror to heat gases.

Navigation

- **Early sailors** found their way by staying near land, looking for "landmarks" on shore. Away from land they steered by stars, so had only a vague idea of direction in the day.

- **After c.1100** European sailors used a magnetic compass to find North.

- **A compass** only gives you a direction to steer; it does not tell you where you are.

- **The astrolabe** was used from c.1350. This measured the angle of a star, or the Sun at noon so gave a rough idea of latitude (how far north or south of the Equator).

- **From the 1500s** the cross staff gave a more accurate measure of latitude at night from the angle between the Pole Star and the horizon.

- **From the mid-1700s** until the 1950s, sailors measured latitude with a mirror sextant. This had two mirrors. It gave the angle of a star (including the Sun) when one

◀ *A navigational instrument for measuring latitude from the angle of certain stars.*

mirror was adjusted until the star was at horizon height in the other.

- **For centuries** the only way to find longitude—how far east or west—was by dead reckoning. This meant trailing a knotted rope in the water to keep track of speed and estimate how far you had come.

- **You can find longitude** by comparing the Sun's height with its height at the same time at a longitude you know. But early pendulum clocks did not work well enough aboard ship to give the correct time.

- **The longitude problem** was solved in the 1700s, when John Harrison made a very accurate spring-driven clock, or chronometer.

- **Ships** can now find their position with pinpoint accuracy using the Global Positioning System (GPS). This works by electronically comparing signals from a ring of satellites.

Sydney Opera House

▲ *Standing by the water's edge in Sydney Harbour, Sydney Opera House is one of the world's most distinctive buildings.*

- **Sydney Opera House** in Sydney, opened in October 1973, is one of Australia's best known landmarks.

- **The design** by Danish architect Jorn Utzon was agreed after a competition involving 233 entries, but it took 14 years to build.

- **The radical sail-like** roofs were said to have been inspired by seashells.

- **The original design** was so unusual that it proved impossible to build structurally, so Utzon altered the shape of the roofs to base them on sections of a ball.

- **The altered design** meant the roofs could be made from precast concrete slabs.

- **The roofs** were made from 2,194 precast concrete slabs, weighing up to 15 tons each.

- **The slabs** are tied together with 220mi (350km) of tensioned steel cable and covered with one million Swedish tiles.

- **In the mouths of the roofs** are 67,000 sq ft (6,225 sq m) of double layered French glass.

- **Inside,** there were originally four theaters: the Concert Hall, the Opera Theater, the Drama Theater, and the Playhouse.

- **A new theater,** the Studio, was added in March 1999.

Bombers of World War II

- **In the 1930s** Boeing built the B-17 *Flying Fortress*, bristling with gun turrets to battle its way through to targets, even by day.

- **The 1929** Curtis F8C Helldiver was the first "dive bomber," designed to drop bombs at the end of a dive on targets like aircraft carriers. German "Stuka" dive bombers gained a fearsome name in the German invasions of 1939.

- **The twin-engined** Heinkel 111, Dornier Do17, and Junkers Ju88 were the main German bombers in the *Blitzkrieg* (literally "lightning war") raids of the Battle of Britain.

- **In December 1939** the heavy loss of British Wellingtons showed that lightly armed bombers could not sustain daylight raids, so the British switched to night raids.

- **Blind bombing** radar systems like the Hs2, and flare trails left by advance "Pathfinder" missions, improved accuracy on night raids.

- ◀ *The British Avro Lancaster could carry 6.6 tons of bombs on low altitude raids.*

- **The ultralight** De Havilland Mosquito was fast enough to fly daylight raids.

- **The Russian Ilyushin Il-2** or Stormovik was so good at bombing tanks Stalin said it was "as necessary to the Red Army as air or bread."

- **The dambusters** were the Lancasters of 617 squadron of 1943 that attacked German dams with "bouncing bombs." These were round bombs designed by Barnes Wallis that bounced over the water toward the dams.

- **Kamikaze** (Japanese for "divine wind") were fighters loaded with bombs and gasoline which their pilots aimed in suicide dives at enemy ships.

- **The biggest bomber** was the Boeing B-29 Superfortress. It could fly over 32,000ft (10,000m) up. In 1945, it dropped atomic bombs on Hiroshima and Nagasaki in Japan.

Early cars

- **In 1890** Frenchman Emile Levassor made the first car with an engine at the front. He laughed, saying, "C'est brutal, mais ça marche" ("It's rough, but it goes").

- **The Duryea** brothers made the first successful American car in 1893.

- **Until 1896** in Britain and 1901 in New York cars had to be preceded by a man on foot waving a red flag.

- **In 1895** the French Panhard-Levassor company made the first covered "saloon" car.

- **In 1898** Renault drove the wheels with a shaft not a chain.

- **The Oldsmobile** Curved Dash of 1900 was the first car to sell in thousands.

- **On early cars** speed was controlled by moving a small ignition advance lever backward or forward.

- **Dirt roads,** oil spray, and noise meant early motorists needed protective clothing such as goggles.

- **The first cars** had wooden or wire spoked wheels. Pressed steel wheels like today's came in after 1945.

- **In 1906** an American steam-driven car, the Stanley Steamer, broke the land speed record at over 127mph (205km/h).

◀ *By 1904, many cars were starting to have the familiar layout of cars today—engine at the front, driver on one side, steering wheel, gas tank at the back, a shaft to drive the wheels, and so on.*

Canals

- **In 1470BC** the Egyptian Pharaoh Sesostris had the first Suez Canal built, linking the Mediterranean and Red Sea.

- **The Grand Canal** in China is the world's longest manufactured waterway, running 1,085mi (1,747km).

- **The origins** of the Grand Canal date to the 4th century BC, but it was rebuilt in AD607.

- **The late 1700s and early 1800s** saw many canals built for the factories of the Industrial Revolution, like James Brindley's Bridgwater Canal in Lancashire, England.

- **Clinton's Folly** is the Erie Canal linking Lake Erie to the Hudson, organized by governor De Witt Clinton in 1825.

- **The current Suez Canal** was built by Ferdinand de Lesseps (1859–69). It is the world's longest big-ship canal, 100.59mi (161.9km) long.

- **The Panama canal** links the Atlantic and Pacific Oceans 100mi (82km) across Central America. It cuts the ocean voyage from New York to San Francisco by 8,948mi (14,400km).

▲ Amsterdam's canals were dug in the city's heyday in the 1600s.

- **The Panama Canal** takes over 400 million tons of shipping a year.

- **The world's busiest canal** is Germany's Kiel which takes 4,500 ships a year from the North Sea to the Baltic.

- **In Russia** one of the world's longest canal systems links the Black Sea to the Arctic Ocean via the Volga River.

Airliners

- **The Boeing 247** of 1933 was the world's first modern airliner, with monoplane wings and streamlined body.

- **The Douglas DC-3** of 1936 could carry 21 passengers at 200mph (320km/h) and was the first popular airliner.

- **In 1952** the world's first jet airliner, the De Havilland Comet came into service.

- **The Comet** more than halved international flight times, but several tragic accidents led to its grounding in 1954. It flew again in 1958.

> **! NEWS FLASH !**
> Spaceplanes like Lockheed-Martin's *Venture Star* may make space trips routine flights.

- **The age of jet** air travel really began with the American Boeing 707 and Douglas DC-8 of the late 1950s.

- **The Boeing 747** jumbo jet of 1970 had over 400 seats, making air travel cheaper.

- **Four-engined jets** like the 747 can fly 6,000mi (10,000km) nonstop at speeds of 620mph (1,000km/h).

- **Supersonic airliners** able to travel at over 1,250mph (2,000km/h) like the Anglo-French Concorde and Russian Tupolev Tu-144 have proved too heavy on fuel and too noisy. Only a few have been built.

- **The 555-seat Airbus** A380 will be the first full-length double deck airliner.

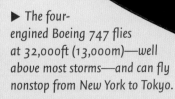

▶ The four-engined Boeing 747 flies at 32,000ft (13,000m)—well above most storms—and can fly nonstop from New York to Tokyo.

INDEX

Acknowledgments

Artists: Terry Riley, Peter Sarson

The publishers would like to thank the following sources for the photographs used in this book:

Page 9 (T/R) CORBIS; Page 11 (T/L) Steve Lindridge, Eye Ubiquitous/CORBIS; Page 14 (B/L) Richard T. Nowitz/CORBIS;
Page 25 (B/L) CORBIS; Page 38 (B/L) Jim Sugar Photography/CORBIS; Page 41 (B/R) Joseph Sohm, ChromoSohm Inc./CORBIS;
Page 43 (T/R) In-press photography; Page 49 (T/R) Wolfgang Kaehler/CORBIS

All other photographs are from MKP Archives